The Gift of Guests

Lessons in Hospitality, Faith, and Becoming Human Together

Joel Vestal

Zaydaya Press

Some names and identifying details have been changed to protect the privacy of individuals.

Published by Zaydaya Press

United States of America

First Edition, 2025

For all the brave souls and friends I have met from around the world.

Your lives have inspired me and made me a better person.

Shukran — Arabic

Ce zu tin ba — Burmese

Khob khun — Thai

Gracias — Spanish

Murakoze — Kinyarwanda

Asante — Swahili

Mahadsanid — Somali

Merci — French

Tashakor — Pashto

Contents

Introduction

"The stranger at your door is rarely just a stranger. They are an invitation to become someone you have not yet been."

For the past ten years, I have had the privilege of walking alongside immigrants and refugees. It has been one of the great gifts of my life. It has also been challenging, humbling, and deeply formative. This book is not the product of a strategy or a theory, but the outgrowth of relationships—of encounters, conversations, and shared moments that have shaped me in ways I did not expect. I did not come to this work as an expert. I came as a neighbor, and eventually, as a friend. I came with good intentions, which is both a starting point and, I have learned, a very thin foundation on its own. Good intentions get you to the door. But what happens after you walk through requires something more: a willingness to be surprised, to sit with discomfort, and to allow your assumptions to be quietly dismantled by people whose lives do not fit your categories. Again and again, I have found myself changed by the people I was supposed to be helping. Through their stories, I have learned about forgiveness that refuses bitterness, listening that crosses difference, vulnerability practiced under pressure, dignity honored in small things, hope that grows slowly, belonging forged through consistency, burdens shared when life becomes heavy, hospitality offered without abundance, faith refined by suffering, and leadership rooted in resilience. I did not set out to write a book. For years, these stories simply accumulated—in car rides, in waiting rooms, in conversations over food, in moments of crisis and moments of unexpected joy. I carried them around the way you carry something valuable that you're not sure what to do with. Eventually I realized I couldn't keep them to myself. They belonged to a wider conversation. Let me be honest about what this book is and what it is not. It is not a policy argument. I will not spend these pages debating border security or immigration law, though I believe those conversations matter and deserve serious attention. This book lives at a different level—the level of the human, the particular, the relational. It is about what happens when two people from very different worlds choose to see each other. It is also not a book about me rescuing anyone. If anything, it is the opposite. The pattern that kept repeating itself, chapter after chapter, year after year, was this: I would show up thinking I was the one with something to offer, and I would leave having received far more than I gave. I am not sure I have fully made peace with that reversal. But I have stopped being surprised by it. This book is an invitation—to slow down, to pay attention, and to grow in our capacity to love. It is written for people of faith who want to live with greater hospitality toward those who are different, who come from other places, and who carry stories we may not yet understand. But it is also written for anyone who has sensed that something essential is missing in how we live together—some quality of presence, attention, and mutual care that our busy, defended lives have quietly eroded. Each chapter centers on a person or a moment. These are not composite characters or illustrative fictions. They are real people, real conversations, real cars on real roads in real cities. I have changed some names and identifying details to protect privacy, but the substance of what happened, what was said, and what I learned is as true as I can make it. My hope is that these lessons, received as gifts, will help all of us become more human together. Not more comfortable. Not more certain. But more human. That, I have come to believe, is enough of a goal for one book—and perhaps for one lifetime.

Chapter 1

Forgiveness as a Gift

When the Wounded Teach Forgiveness

"The world changes every time a human being is seen instead of feared."

Armand had been in the United States for six months. Six months since arriving through the refugee resettlement process. Six months of learning a new city, a new language, a new rhythm of life. Six months of working nights, trying to steady himself in a place that still felt unfamiliar, still uncertain. He was doing what so many newcomers do—keeping his head down, showing up to work, trusting that if he did the right things long enough, life would eventually begin to settle. It was around three in the morning when it happened. Armand was walking home from work when he was attacked. Someone struck him over the head, hard enough to send him to the ground. They took his car and left him injured in the dark. By the time I heard from him, the night had already turned into a blur of police reports, emergency rooms, and confusion spoken in a language he was still learning to navigate.

When Armand called me later that day, he had already been stitched up and released from the ER. His head was sore. His body was exhausted. And he was trying to figure out what to do next. He didn't know where his car was. He didn't know how to recover it. He didn't know how any of this worked. What he knew was that he needed help. The police had eventually located the car and had it towed to an impound lot. It was there—but getting it back meant paperwork, directions, fees, and conversations that felt overwhelming when your head is still throbbing and your confidence is thin. So I picked him up the next day to drive him to retrieve it. His wife came with us. We sat together in the car—three people moving through a city that felt ordinary to me and anything but ordinary to them. I was angry. Not the loud kind of anger, but the tight, protective kind that settles in your chest and refuses to loosen. The kind that shows up when someone you care about has been violated and you can't fix it. Armand had done everything right. He was working. He was staying out of trouble. He was new, vulnerable, still learning the rules. And this was how he was welcomed. The car was quiet as we drove. At some point, Armand spoke. 'I will forgive them,' he said.

The words were simple. Measured. Spoken without drama. I didn't respond right away. I wasn't sure how to receive that sentence. Forgiveness felt too soon, too tidy for what had happened. My instinct was to protect him—not just physically, but emotionally. I wanted space for his anger. I wanted outrage on his behalf. I wanted justice to come first. Before I could say anything, his wife spoke up. 'I will not forgive them,' she said. Her voice was firm. She was angry. And she made no attempt to soften it.

Her response made immediate sense to me. Someone had hurt her husband. Someone had shattered what little sense of safety they had begun to build. Her anger didn't feel like a failure. It felt like love trying to find its footing in a moment of shock. And suddenly, without planning it, a conversation opened up in the car. It wasn't polished. English is not their first language, and the vocabulary was limited. We spoke slowly. Carefully. Sometimes repeating ourselves. Sometimes reaching for words that weren't quite there yet. What does it mean to forgive? Is forgiveness the same as saying what happened was okay? Does forgiving mean you stop caring about justice? What happens to a person who holds anger too tightly?

No one was preaching. No one was winning an argument. We were simply trying to name something real together. Armand explained that he did not forgive because the harm was small. He forgave because he did not want to carry it. He had already carried too much in his life—too much loss, too much disruption, too much fear. He did not want this violence to become another weight shaping who he was. His wife listened, but she did not agree. Not yet. And that mattered. ——— Forgiveness was not being demanded. It was not being forced. It was being named as a choice—one that costs something different for each person who considers it. As I drove, I realized how uncomfortable I felt—not because of their disagreement, but because of what it revealed in me. I had thought of forgiveness primarily as a moral virtue, something admirable, something to aspire to once emotions have settled and clarity has returned. But Armand was not speaking from comfort or distance. He was speaking from experience. He understood something I had not been required to understand. Forgiveness, for him, was not about being noble. It was about survival. About refusing to let violence shape the rest of his story. About deciding, even while wounded, what kind of person he would become next.

His wife's anger was also real. It came from fear. From love. From the shock of realizing how exposed they still were in this new place. Her refusal to forgive did not feel like moral failure. It felt like grief that had not yet found words. And somehow, in that small car, with limited language and raw emotion, there was room for all of it. By the time we arrived at the police lot, practical concerns took over. Forms. Fees. Signatures. The slow work of reclaiming what had been taken. But something in me had shifted. I had come to help Armand retrieve his car. I left realizing I had been given something else. I often hear immigrants spoken about as people in need—people to be helped, supported, fixed, or managed. And while need is real, it is not the whole story. What is less often acknowledged is the wisdom that grows in people who have been forced to navigate loss, uncertainty, and injustice long before they ever arrive here. Armand did not offer me a theory of forgiveness. He showed me what it looks like when forgiveness is costly, chosen early, and spoken without guarantees. He reminded me that some of the deepest truths about faith, resilience, and mercy are not learned in safety, but in vulnerability. I still think about that drive—about the stitches in his head, about his wife's anger, about the quiet authority of his words, and about how easily I had assumed I was there only to give help, not to receive it.

If immigrants are a gift—and I believe they are—it is not because they confirm our generosity. It is because they reveal the thin places in our understanding. They show us what words like forgiveness, courage, and hope look like when they are lived under pressure rather than discussed in theory. I've thought about that car ride many times since. Not only about Armand's words, but about what forgiveness has looked like in my own life. I've learned that forgiveness is rarely a single decision that settles everything. It's more like a practice you return to—sometimes daily, sometimes reluctantly, often imperfectly. Forgiveness isn't like getting a flu shot. You don't receive it once and walk away immune to pain. When you've been hurt, the memory has a way of resurfacing. Something reminds you—a tone of voice, a place, a moment—and suddenly you realize you're being asked to forgive again. Not because the first attempt was insincere, but because healing doesn't move in straight lines. That's something

Armand seemed to understand instinctively. His forgiveness wasn't dramatic or final. It was simply the choice he made that day not to let violence take up permanent residence inside him. I've had to learn that same rhythm more slowly. There are seasons when forgiveness feels settled, and others when it feels fragile and incomplete. Sometimes forgiveness looks like compassion. Other times it looks like boundaries. And sometimes it looks like naming the anger honestly before you can release it. Somewhere along the way I came to understand that forgiveness is really about releasing the hope that the past could have been any different. I have found that to be both freeing and deeply challenging. It requires a kind of surrender — not only of the offense itself, but of the version of the story where things turned out the way we wanted them to. Practicing forgiveness, for me, has rarely been heroic. It's usually quiet. Unimpressive. Repetitive. It's choosing, again and again, not to let an old wound dictate a new moment. For those who find forgiveness difficult—and I suspect that is most of us—I don't think the question is, 'Can I forgive?' The better question might be, 'What is one small way I can refuse to be shaped by this hurt today?' Sometimes that looks like releasing the urge to rehearse the story once more. Sometimes it looks like speaking the truth out loud instead of burying it. Sometimes it looks like asking for help because forgiveness feels too heavy to carry alone. What Armand offered me that day was not a formula. It was permission—to see forgiveness as something lived, not mastered. Something practiced, not perfected. And maybe that is part of the gift immigrants offer us—not because they forgive more easily, but because they often forgive more honestly. They remind us that forgiveness is not a finish line. It is a way of walking forward without letting the past decide who we become.

I don't know if I would have forgiven as Armand did. I hope I would. But I also know I have not yet been asked to forgive at that cost. What I do know is this: when forgiveness is spoken by someone who has every reason to withhold it, it sounds different. It carries weight. It demands humility from the listener. And perhaps that is where learning begins—not when we decide to help, but when we are willing to be taught.

Chapter 2

Learning to Listen

When Our Assumptions Are Exposed

"In an age of outrage, tenderness becomes a form of courage."

The question was asked casually. Not dramatically. Not with complaint or bitterness. Just curiosity. An African refugee family, who had been in the United States for several years, asked someone from our team, 'Have you ever been to McDonald's? We heard it was really nice.' When I first heard that question, I didn't know how to respond—not outwardly, but inwardly. Something in me stalled. The words landed heavier than they were meant to. McDonald's. A place so ordinary, so familiar, that many of us don't even register it as a destination. A place associated with convenience, routine, sometimes even indifference. And yet, for this family, it carried a sense of wonder. It wasn't that they wanted fast food. It was that they wanted to understand the place they now lived.

That simple question quietly unraveled a set of assumptions I hadn't realized I was carrying. I had assumed familiarity. I had assumed access. I had assumed that simply being in America meant knowing America. But knowing a place and living in it are not the same thing. For this family, life had narrowed considerably since arriving. Work, home, school, responsibilities. Survival takes up space. Exploration requires margin—and margin is often the last thing newcomers are afforded. What struck me most was not what they lacked, but what they hadn't lost. They still had curiosity. They were still imagining. Still wondering. Still asking questions without embarrassment or apology. ——— That kind of openness is fragile. It can be flattened quickly by disappointment or exclusion. But here it was—alive, intact, and offered freely. As I reflected on that moment, I began to notice how often we confuse presence with participation. We assume that people who live among us share our experiences, our reference points, our sense of what is normal. But for many immigrants, daily life is consumed with adaptation—learning systems, navigating language, figuring out how things work without drawing attention to yourself.

Joy becomes something postponed. Exploration becomes something deferred. And yet, in this simple question, I was reminded that imagination survives even when options are limited. Over time, I began to recognize this pattern again and again. I thought of Jeanne, an adult English learner who laughed with delight when she learned the word staycation. She had never taken a vacation outside of Indianapolis since arriving from a refugee camp. Rest, for her, was not a destination—it was an idea still being learned. I thought of teenagers attending their first baseball game, eyes wide, absorbing something many of us had long stopped noticing. I thought of families experiencing their first restaurant, first park, first public celebration—not as consumers, but as observers trying to understand the rhythms of this place they now called home. These moments were not marked by complaint. They were marked by attentiveness. What began to unsettle me was how rarely I approached my own life with that same posture. Familiarity had dulled my curiosity. Access had replaced wonder. I moved through spaces assuming I understood them simply because I belonged. But belonging is not the same as understanding. Immigrants often see what the rest of us overlook—not because they are wiser by nature, but because they are paying attention. They are reading the culture the way you read a text in a language you are still learning—slowly, carefully, with intention. That kind of attentiveness carries wisdom. The McDonald's question exposed something else as well: how quietly our assumptions about abundance operate. We imagine opportunity as automatic. We assume access is obvious. We forget how much of what we call normal requires time, confidence, and permission. We rarely ask whether people feel welcome enough to explore—or whether survival has narrowed their world to the essentials. What that family offered me was not a critique of America. It was a mirror. It showed me how easily I confuse proximity with belonging. How quickly I assume that people who live among us experience life the way I do. And how rarely I slow down long enough to ask what their world actually looks like from the inside. This is one of the gifts immigrants offer us if we are willing to receive it: they teach us how to see again. They remind us that wonder is not naïve. That curiosity is not weakness. That questions can be a form of hope. That question—'Have you ever been to

McDonald's?'—stayed with me not only because of what it revealed about assumptions, but because of how it was offered. It wasn't confrontational. It wasn't defensive. It wasn't trying to make a point. It was simply asked.

In a world that feels increasingly loud, that kind of curiosity feels rare. We live in a time when conversations are often shaped by urgency—the need to respond quickly, to explain ourselves, to make sure our position is clear. Listening becomes secondary, something we do only long enough to prepare our next sentence. And yet, the stories that have shaped me most—especially in my work with immigrants—have come not from speaking, but from listening long enough to be surprised. There's an old saying that we were given two ears and one mouth for a reason. Whether or not we take it literally, the wisdom still holds. Listening is not passive. It's an active discipline. It requires restraint. It asks us to slow the reflex to correct, defend, or persuade. What I've learned over years of crossing cultural distance is that the first layer of what someone says is rarely the whole story. Meaning is layered. Context is invisible to outsiders. A question that sounds simple—like a question about a fast-food restaurant—can carry within it months of isolation, longing for normalcy, and the courage it took to finally ask someone something personal. When we rush past the surface, we miss what's underneath. And what's underneath is usually what matters. I've also learned that listening is not a neutral act. It is a declaration of value. When I slow down long enough to hear someone fully—to ask a follow-up question, to sit in silence after they've finished rather than immediately filling the air—I am communicating something beyond words. I am saying: you are worth my attention. Your experience is real. You don't have to compress your story to make it easier for me. That communication lands differently for people who have spent years feeling invisible. In a divided city, a divided nation, and a divided world, listening may be one of the most countercultural practices we have left. What I've learned is that listening does not mean agreement. It means presence. It means allowing someone else's experience to exist without immediately measuring it against our own. It means recognizing that understanding usually comes after patience, not before. Immigrants have taught me this repeatedly—not through lectures, but through the way they tell their stories. Often haltingly.

Sometimes indirectly.

Occasionally through questions instead of conclusions. Their words ask something of the listener: attention without interruption. If we want to grow our capacity to listen—for the sake of decency, respect, and dignity—we have to practice it deliberately. Listening without trying to manage the outcome. Listening past our discomfort. Listening in ordinary places, not just moments of crisis. Listening without speaking on behalf of others.

These are not dramatic acts. They are quiet choices that shape how we live together. Listening, at its best, is not about winning an argument or resolving a disagreement. It is about making cooperation possible in a world that would rather fracture. It is about creating space where dignity can survive even when consensus does not. The question about McDonald's did not solve a problem. It did something quieter and more lasting. It changed how I listened. If immigrants are a gift—and I believe they are—it is not because they arrive with answers. It is because they arrive with questions that expose the limits of our certainty and invite us into humility. Sometimes the most profound lessons do not come wrapped in tragedy or heroism. Sometimes they arrive disguised as curiosity, offered gently, waiting to see whether we will dismiss them—or allow them to teach us how to listen again.

Chapter 3

The Courage to Be Vulnerable

The Courage to Be Seen

Thomas called me because he had a warrant out for his arrest. It wasn't for anything dramatic. No violence. No headlines. Just a series of traffic violations that had compounded over time until they became something he could no longer ignore. But when he called, his voice carried the weight of more than paperwork. He wanted me to drive him to turn himself in. There was a long pause after he said it—the kind that leaves room for reconsideration. He could have avoided it longer. Many people do. He could have hoped it would disappear, or worked around it until something forced the issue. Instead, he chose to face it. That choice mattered. Thomas had been in the United States for about ten years. His family arrived when he was twelve. He was twenty-two now—old enough to carry responsibility, young enough to still be learning how consequences work in a system that had never been explained to him clearly. Like many immigrants who arrive as adolescents, he grew up translating not only language, but expectations—figuring things out as he went, often without a map. When I picked him up, he didn't say much at first. His leg bounced nervously as we drove. His eyes stayed fixed on the road ahead, as if keeping them there might steady what he was feeling inside. He didn't know if he would be released the same day. He didn't know if he would be held overnight. He didn't know what would happen next. What he knew was that he didn't want to keep running. At one point, as we sat in the car, I noticed the tattoo on his arm—a simple image of Jesus. It wasn't new. It looked like something he had chosen years earlier, when faith still felt more certain and decisions less complicated. We talked quietly. Not in speeches. Not in slogans. Just honest conversation about choices, consequences, and the fear that comes when you realize a decision can no longer be postponed. Thomas wasn't asking for reassurance. He wasn't asking me to tell him everything would be fine. What he wanted was something simpler and harder: someone to sit with him in the uncertainty. ——— Vulnerability has a way of doing that. It strips away performance. There's no room for bravado when you're about to walk into a place where control ends and waiting begins.

When we arrived, Thomas took a deep breath. He said something quietly—more like a confession than a statement. He wanted his life to move in a better direction, even if the next step was painful. Then he got out of the car. I watched him walk inside, aware that I couldn't follow him where he was going. I didn't know how long he would be held. I didn't know how this would affect his job, his family, or his sense of stability. All I could do was wait—and eventually, leave him there. That was the hardest part. There's a temptation, especially in conversations about immigrants, to rush into defense—to clarify that this doesn't represent everyone, or to insist that most immigrants are law-abiding. While those statements may be true, they can miss something deeper. Thomas was not defined by his mistake. He was defined by how he chose to face it. Vulnerability is rarely celebrated in public life. We admire confidence, certainty, control. But vulnerability—real vulnerability—requires a different kind of courage. It asks us to admit fear. To accept consequences. To be seen not as we wish we were, but as we are. That day, Thomas taught me that vulnerability is not weakness. It is the moment when growth becomes possible. As I reflected on that experience, I began to notice that Thomas's courage was not an isolated event. It was part of a larger pattern I kept encountering as I walked alongside immigrants and refugees. Again and again, I saw people risk being seen. Sometimes it was dramatic, like Thomas choosing accountability over avoidance.

Other times it was quiet—asking for help with paperwork, admitting confusion about systems they didn't understand, naming fear without knowing how it would be received. One of our volunteers once sat in a hospital waiting room with a woman whose husband was dying. The woman looked at her and said simply, 'My God left me.' There was no anger in her voice—only exhaustion. She wasn't asking for an explanation. She wasn't looking for a lesson. She was trusting someone with her truth. That moment stayed with me, even though I wasn't the one sitting there. It reminded me how much vulnerability asks of the listener. It requires presence without fixing. Patience without answers. The courage to let honesty exist without rushing it toward resolution. I saw that same courage when young people returned to community after long absences, unsure if they still belonged. When someone admitted a mistake that carried consequences. When a family chose honesty even though it might cost them stability. These were not moments of weakness. They were moments of alignment—when people chose integrity over image.

Over time, vulnerability began to teach me something about myself. I realized how carefully I managed my own appearance. How often I avoided discomfort by staying competent. How rarely I allowed myself to be seen when I didn't know what to do next. Being close to immigrants disrupted that. Their willingness to name uncertainty exposed how often I hid mine. There is something particularly exposing about sitting with someone whose vulnerability is not a choice—it has been imposed on them by circumstance, by systems, by the bare fact of being new and unknown in a place where everyone else already has a map. When you watch someone carry that kind of involuntary exposure with grace, it becomes harder to justify your own carefully constructed defenses. I think about the armor I wear in ordinary life. The polish of competence. The instinct to have an answer ready. The reflex to minimize my own confusion or fear before it can be noticed. These habits feel like professionalism, but they are often just self-protection. And there is a cost to them—not only to me, but to the people around me who might be waiting for someone to go first. Thomas didn't become courageous when he walked into that jail. He became courageous when he admitted he needed help getting there. That distinction changed me.

Vulnerability, I learned, is not about exposure for its own sake. It's about choosing honesty when avoidance would be easier. It's about letting go of the illusion that strength means self-sufficiency. In a culture that rewards confidence and control, vulnerability is often misread as failure. But what I encountered told a different story. Vulnerability was strength practiced without armor. Courage without applause. And it was contagious. If immigrants are a gift—and I believe they are—it is because they invite us into a fuller way of living. One where dignity is not tied to perfection. Where responsibility and compassion are not opposites. Where growth begins not with certainty, but with truth. For readers who want to practice vulnerability in their own lives, the invitation is not dramatic. It may look like admitting you don't have the answer. Owning a mistake without excuses. Asking for help before things fall apart. Staying present when someone shares pain instead of trying to solve it. Vulnerability does not eliminate fear. It walks through it. And in a divided world—where people are reduced to categories, headlines, and assumptions—vulnerability may be one of the most humanizing forces we have left. It refuses to let people become caricatures. It insists on complexity. It makes room for change.

Walking alongside immigrants has taught me this again and again: the people we are tempted to see as threats are often our teachers. Not because they are flawless, but because they are willing to be honest. Thomas walked into that building unsure of what would happen next. But he walked in whole. And sometimes, that is the bravest thing a person can do.

Chapter 4

Dignity in the Small Things

The first thing I noticed was the floor. Not because it was dirty or unfinished, but because it was where he slept. The mattress lay directly on the ground, thin and worn, pushed into the corner of a room that held very little else. No bed frame. No headboard. No sense that this was temporary. This was simply how things were. He was a refugee teenager—old enough to carry himself with quiet self-awareness, young enough not to complain. When I asked where he slept, he answered plainly, without embarrassment. There was no story attached to it. No apology. No explanation. This was normal to him. That's what stayed with me. Not the absence of a bed, but how easily deprivation had settled into the shape of everyday life. How quickly something that should have stood out had become invisible—not only to him, but to the systems and people around him. There was no crisis. No emergency. No moment that demanded immediate intervention. Just a quiet erosion of dignity that had gone unnoticed because it didn't announce itself.

We often imagine dignity being threatened in dramatic ways—through violence, discrimination, or public humiliation. But more often, dignity is diminished through small omissions. Through what is missing. Through what is quietly accepted as 'good enough.' A bed is not a luxury. It is not excess. It is not something earned by success. It is a place to rest. A signal that your body matters. A way of saying that comfort and stability are not reserved for some, but belong to all. That moment reshaped how I understood dignity. It also reshaped how I understood judgment. ——— I realized how easily we assess people's situations without ever asking how they came to be that way. How quickly we grow cynical—assuming laziness, poor choices, or lack of effort—when the truth is often far more complex and far more human. The mattress on the floor wasn't evidence of failure. It was evidence of survival. Once I began to see this, I couldn't stop seeing it. I thought of a refugee girl who received her first pair of glasses after years of squinting through classrooms and streets. She didn't know that people could see that clearly. When she put them on, the world sharpened—not just visually, but emotionally. Her posture changed. Her confidence shifted. She hadn't known what she was missing, only that learning had always felt harder than it seemed to be for others. That wasn't charity. That was dignity being restored. I thought of a refugee high school senior preparing for prom. The dress mattered, yes—but what mattered more was what the dress represented. Belonging. Being seen. Being able to participate in a shared milestone rather than standing quietly on the edges of it. Covering the ticket. Helping with a manicure. Making sure she could show up fully. These weren't indulgences. They were affirmations. Again and again, I watched refugees encounter the same unspoken barrier—not overt rejection, but lowered expectations. The assumption that comfort, celebration, and ease were optional. That survival was enough. But survival is not the same as dignity. Dignity is being able to rest. To see clearly. To celebrate. To belong. What unsettled me most was how easy it is to stop noticing these things. How quickly we say, 'At least they're safe,' as if safety alone is the goal. How often judgment creeps in—not loudly, but quietly—shaping how we talk, how we vote, how we decide who is 'deserving.' There is a particular cruelty in the word deserving when it is applied to basic human needs. A child does not deserve a warm place to sleep because they have earned it. They deserve it because they are a child. A person does not deserve medical care because they have proven their worth. They deserve it because they are a person. Dignity is not a reward. It is a starting condition. But we forget this. Our systems forget it too. And in the forgetting, we build structures that sort people into tiers—the deserving and the undeserving, the productive and the dependent, the ones who get the bed frame and the ones who sleep on the floor. Refugees didn't choose those tiers. They arrived in them. Cynicism grows when we stop seeing people as whole. Being close to refugees disrupted that in me. It forced me to confront how often I had confused my own comfort with moral clarity. How quickly I labeled something as unnecessary simply because I had never gone without it. The bed on the floor became a teacher. It taught me that dignity is rarely restored through sweeping solutions. More often, it is restored through attention—through noticing what has quietly gone without, and refusing to look away. I've thought often about the small gestures I witnessed that carried enormous weight. A volunteer who noticed a family had no curtains and quietly brought some over. A teacher who made sure a student had the same supplies as every other student. A neighbor who learned a family's names and used them. None of these made the news. None of them solved poverty or resolved immigration backlogs or changed policy. But each of them communicated something that policy alone cannot communicate: you are seen. You matter. Your comfort is not incidental. That communication is not small. For someone who has spent months or years feeling invisible, it is immense. Refugees did not demand this lesson. They lived it. That is part of the gift they offer—if we are willing to receive it. For readers who want to grow in recognizing dignity in the small things, the invitation begins with restraint. Restrain the impulse to judge before you understand. Restrain the habit of assuming you know someone's story. Restrain the cynicism that flattens complex lives into simple explanations. Instead, practice curiosity. Ask what feels normal to you but may be missing for someone else. Notice what people adapt to without complaint. Pay attention to what has been quietly endured rather than loudly protested. Dignity grows when we stop asking only, 'Are they okay?' and begin asking, 'What would help them live fully?' The mattress on the floor was not a tragedy. But it was a warning. It warned me how easy it is to overlook what matters most. How quickly we can grow accustomed to absence. How dangerous it is to let judgment replace attention. If refugees are a gift—and I believe they are—it is because they help us recover our sight. They show us that a better way of living does not begin with suspicion or critique, but with care. With seeing. With refusing to let small indignities pass unnoticed. Sometimes dignity is restored through policy. Sometimes through programs. And sometimes, it begins with something as small—and as profound—as a bed lifted off the floor.

Chapter 5

Slow Hope

Uwase laughed when she learned the word staycation. The conversation happened while she was working with one of our volunteers. It was casual—one of those ordinary exchanges that doesn't announce itself as important until later. Someone mentioned taking time off, resting without leaving town, and the word surfaced naturally, as if it were something everyone understood. Uwase paused.

She repeated it slowly—staycation—testing the sound of it, then laughed. Not because it was funny, but because it was unfamiliar. The idea itself seemed almost foreign: taking time to rest without going anywhere, choosing stillness rather than necessity. Uwase was a single mother raising two daughters. Since arriving in the United States as a refugee, she had been doing what survival required—working long hours, stretching limited resources, learning a new language, and navigating systems that rarely explain themselves clearly. One of her daughters had special needs, which added another layer of complexity to every decision, every schedule, every form. Money was always tight. Time even tighter. She had never taken a vacation. Not outside the city. Not inside it either, really. Rest, for her, was not something you planned. It was something that happened only when nothing else demanded attention—which was rare. Her laughter wasn't bitter. It wasn't resentful. It was simply honest. When the volunteer later shared that moment with me, it stayed with me longer than I expected. Not because of what Uwase said, but because of what the word revealed. It revealed how quickly people learn to live without rest when survival requires it. How endurance becomes normal. How waiting stretches long enough that hope must change its shape in order to survive. Uwase's life had been interrupted by forces far beyond her control—war, displacement, the loss of home and familiarity. Like many refugees, her story included ruptures that no one chooses and no one forgets. And yet, what struck me was not the scale of her loss, but the steadiness of her presence. She didn't speak often about what had been taken. She spoke about what was necessary. About what still needed to be done. About tomorrow. There is a kind of hope that survives only because it learns how to be patient. We often imagine hope as something bright and forward-moving—an expectation that circumstances will improve quickly, visibly, decisively. When that doesn't happen, we assume hope has failed.

We confuse disappointment with absence. But what I began to learn, again and again, through stories like Uwase's, was that hope does not always look like optimism. Sometimes it looks like endurance. Slow hope is not naïve. It has seen too much for that. It is hope that has been stripped of illusion but not of meaning. Hope that continues even when timelines stretch longer than expected. Hope that adapts without surrendering. As I listened to volunteers share moments like this, I began to notice the same pattern repeating across countless lives. Single parents carrying the weight of entire households alone. Caregivers navigating systems that were not built with their realities in mind. Families waiting years for paperwork to move, for stability to arrive, for life to feel less fragile. In these spaces, hope did not disappear. It learned how to survive without celebration. Without certainty. Without guarantees. What unsettled me most was how uncomfortable this kind of hope made me. I wanted movement. Resolution. Clear evidence that things were getting better. I wanted stories that went somewhere obvious. But slow hope refuses to perform. It does not rush to reassure. It does not pretend the waiting is light. It does not promise outcomes it cannot control. Instead, it stays. Uwase taught me—without trying—that endurance is not the absence of longing. It is the decision to keep showing up even when longing remains unmet. It is the courage to build a life in the meantime.

——— That kind of hope is costly. It asks people to invest in a future they cannot see clearly. To plant roots in uncertain soil. To trust that faithfulness matters even when recognition does not come. To keep choosing care, responsibility, and love even when exhaustion feels constant. And it forced me to examine my own relationship with hope. I realized how much of my hope depended on momentum. On visible progress. On the reassurance that effort would be rewarded within a reasonable timeframe. I had learned to expect change quickly—or to grow frustrated when it didn't arrive. Slow hope challenged that expectation. It suggested that faithfulness might matter more than speed. That staying present, day after day, without guarantees, could still be a meaningful way to live. I think of the farmers in Scripture who do not dig up their seeds to check their progress. They plant, and they water, and they wait—trusting that something is happening underground that their eyes cannot yet see. There is wisdom in that posture that our culture has largely abandoned. We want metrics. We want feedback. We want to know immediately whether our investment is paying off. But some of the most important things in life do not give us that assurance. Raising children. Building friendship. Recovering from loss. Forming faith. These grow on their own timeline, not ours. And the person who cannot wait for them is the person who will never fully have them. Refugees have lived this. Not as a philosophy, but as a daily practice. They know what it is to wait for paperwork, for decisions made by people in offices they will never visit, for security that keeps getting pushed another few months down the road. They have learned to build a life anyway—not because waiting stopped being hard, but because stopping was not an option. For people whose lives have been shattered by war, displacement, and injustice, hope often has to be rebuilt from the ground up. Not as a grand vision, but as a series of small commitments: to work another shift, to advocate for a child, to learn another word, to trust one more neighbor, to believe that tomorrow is still worth preparing for. This kind of hope does not deny grief. It does not erase loss. It does not hurry healing. Instead, it carries grief alongside responsibility. It allows pain to coexist with purpose. It makes room for sorrow without letting sorrow have the final word. Uwase's laughter at the word staycation was not the laughter of someone who had given up. It was the laughter of someone who had adapted so thoroughly that rest had become abstract. Her life had taught her how to endure—but it also revealed how much endurance costs. That realization changed how I think about hope.

Hope is not the belief that things will turn out the way we want. Hope is the decision to keep living faithfully when they don't. Hope is choosing to invest in the future even when the present feels unfinished. Hope is continuing to love, work, and trust without assurance that those efforts will be rewarded quickly. Hope is refusing to let waiting convince you that your life has stalled. This is the hope refugees have shown me again and again—not a loud hope, but a durable one. A hope that survives disruption. A hope that does not depend on speed or certainty. A hope that endures because it has learned how to live with unanswered questions. In a world that demands quick fixes and visible success, slow hope reminds us that some of the most meaningful lives are built patiently, quietly, over time. Uwase may never have taken a vacation. But through her life—and through the quiet wisdom she offered one volunteer in an ordinary conversation—she has taught me something far more lasting. Hope does not have to rush to be real. Sometimes, hope is simply the courage to keep going.

Chapter 6

Belonging

When It Starts to Feel Like Home

It didn't happen all at once. No ribbon cutting. No announcement. No moment where someone stood up and declared that this place had become something more than a program. It happened slowly, almost imperceptibly, through repetition. People kept coming back. CARE Club was never designed to solve loneliness or rebuild community in a fractured world. It was meant to be a space—simple, consistent, open. And yet, over time, something deeper began to form. Students returned after long absences. Some showed up late, tired from work or family responsibilities. Others came early, helping set up chairs or asking if there was anything they could do. A few disappeared for months, only to return quietly, as if testing whether the door was still open. It always was. That's when I began to realize that what was forming here wasn't attraction or entertainment. It was belonging.

———

Belonging shows itself not in excitement, but in commitment. In presence. In the confidence that you can leave and still come back. In a world like ours, that kind of space is rare. We live in a culture more connected than ever—and yet more isolated. We carry entire networks in our pockets, but often don't know the names of the people living next door. We scroll through updates, opinions, and arguments, but struggle to find places where we are known, missed, and welcomed without conditions. Belonging has become fragile in Western society. We move often. We guard ourselves carefully. We trade depth for convenience. We stay busy, but alone. CARE Club quietly disrupted that. James was one of the first people who helped me see it. When he arrived in the United States as a teenage refugee, he spoke very little English. Conversations were halting. School was overwhelming. Everything—from classrooms to grocery stores—required constant interpretation. At CARE Club, he didn't need to explain himself. He showed up. He listened. He stayed. Over time, his confidence grew—not just in language, but in presence. He began to speak more. To laugh. To help others navigate the same confusion he had once carried alone. Years later, James graduated from college. Today, he works, supports himself, and lives with a quiet steadiness that doesn't call attention to itself. When he talks about CARE

Club, he doesn't describe it as a service that helped him succeed. He describes it as a place where he belonged before he had anything to offer. That distinction matters. Belonging did not follow his success. His success followed belonging. Mohammed's story echoes the same truth. He arrived as a refugee with a deep love for soccer and very little certainty about what life in America would hold. CARE Club became one of the first places where he felt seen not as a problem to be solved, but as a person with gifts. People noticed his discipline. His teamwork. His joy. Opportunities followed—not because he was exceptional, but because he was known. Mohammed eventually earned a college scholarship to play soccer. But when he talks about that journey, he doesn't start with the scholarship. He starts with the community that believed in him before his future was clear. Belonging gave him the confidence to risk growth. Then there's Diana. Her story is quieter. No dramatic turning point. No headline moment. She simply kept showing up. She learned. She grew. She found her footing. Today, Diana is doing well—not because she was rescued, but because she was included. CARE Club was not a stepping stone she outgrew; it was a place that helped her become herself. These stories share something essential. Belonging came before achievement. Community came before clarity. Presence came before progress. That's a lesson many of us in Western society have forgotten. We often treat belonging as something you earn—through success, contribution, or alignment. But the spaces that shape us most deeply are the ones that offer belonging first, trusting that growth will follow. Immigrants remember this. Many come from cultures where community is assumed, not negotiated. Where people gather not because it's efficient, but because it's necessary. Where showing up matters more than standing out. When they arrive in a society like ours—fast, individualistic, and achievement-oriented—they often feel the absence of something they can't immediately name. Something is missing in the way people relate. There is warmth but not rootedness. Kindness but not commitment. People are friendly, but the friendship feels shallow, easily dissolved when convenience runs out. CARE Club became a place where that absence was quietly addressed—not through strategy, but through consistency. Belonging grew because the door stayed open. Because names were remembered. Because people were trusted with responsibility.

Because presence mattered more than performance. I have seen belonging form across language barriers, cultural differences, and wildly different life experiences. I have watched people who could barely communicate still find their way to each other through shared space and repeated presence. I have watched trust build not through grand declarations, but through the simple act of showing up again and again. This is not sentimental. It is deeply practical. Trust requires time. Community requires consistency. There is no shortcut. Watching this unfold forced me to confront my own assumptions. I realized how often I confuse welcome with belonging. How easy it is to say, 'You're invited,' while still keeping people at arm's length. How rarely I allow spaces in my own life where someone could disappear and still return without explanation. Belonging requires risk—from everyone involved. It requires letting people shape the space, not just occupy it. It requires patience with difference. It requires resisting the urge to manage outcomes. Immigrants didn't just enter CARE Club. They helped form it. And in doing so, they reminded us of something our society desperately needs to recover: that belonging is not built through perfection or agreement, but through shared life. For readers longing for deeper connection, the invitation of belonging is both simple and demanding. Show up regularly, even when it's inconvenient. Learn names—and remember them. Create spaces where absence doesn't mean exclusion.

Trust people with responsibility, not just attendance. Belonging grows where presence is practiced. CARE Club didn't solve loneliness. But it offered something just as important: a place where people could become known over time. If immigrants are a gift—and I believe they are—it is because they help us remember what we've lost. They remind us that community is not a luxury. It is a necessity. And that belonging, once rediscovered, has the power to reshape not only their lives—but ours. Sometimes home is not a place you arrive at. Sometimes it's a place that waits for you to come back.

Chapter 7

When the Weight Is Shared

Mohammed told the story quietly. There was no drama in his voice, no attempt to impress or explain. It came out the way memories often do when they have been carried for a long time—measured, steady, almost distant. When the bombing began, there was no plan. Only movement. People ran when they could. Those who couldn't were carried. Mohammed's mother couldn't run. So he carried her. They moved through darkness, across land they knew was dangerous but had no choice but to cross. The ground was scattered with landmines—leftovers of a war that did not distinguish between soldiers and families, between past and present. He carried her step by step, knowing that one wrong move could end everything. He did not know how far they would have to go. He did not know if they would survive the night. He only knew that leaving her behind was not an option. When he finished telling the story, there was no moral attached to it. No lesson drawn. It wasn't offered as an example of courage or sacrifice. It was simply part of his life—something he had done because love demanded it. That story stayed with me, not because it was extraordinary, but because it reframed everything I thought I knew about burden. Mohammed did not learn how to carry weight in America. He arrived already knowing how. Later, when I watched Mohammed show up for others—driving someone to an appointment, staying late to help, checking in on people quietly—I began to understand that these actions were not kindness added onto his life. They were continuity. This was how he had survived. This was how he loved. Once I noticed this, I began to see the same pattern everywhere. I saw it in hospital rooms, where refugees took turns staying overnight with someone who wasn't related to them by blood. They slept in chairs, on floors, wherever space allowed. No one asked whose responsibility it was. No one checked schedules. They stayed because leaving felt wrong. In those rooms, care was not transactional. It wasn't organized or efficient. It was relational. Shared. Ordinary. I saw it when families quietly pooled money together for another family facing crisis—rent short, job lost, medical bill arrived. The amounts were often small. No one had much to spare. But together, they made enough. There were no speeches about generosity. No expectation of repayment. Just the understanding that survival had always been communal. ——— These moments stood in sharp contrast to the world many of us inhabit. In Western society, we are taught to carry our burdens privately. Independence is praised. Needing help is framed as failure. Even in moments of deep pain, we often ask, 'How do I manage this?' rather than, 'Who can carry this with me?' We compartmentalize suffering. We rush grief. We apologize for needing others. But the people I was walking alongside knew something different. They had learned—through loss, displacement, and danger—that weight carried alone becomes unbearable. That survival depends on shared responsibility. That love is not proven through words, but through presence when escape would be easier. This does not romanticize suffering. No one I knew wished these lessons upon themselves. They came at terrible cost. But once learned, they shaped how people lived. Watching this changed me. I realized how often I had confused helping with staying. How quickly I looked for solutions instead of companionship. How tempted I was to withdraw when a situation could not be fixed.

But shared burden does not ask for solutions. It asks for commitment. There is a verse in the New Testament that seems almost too simple: 'Carry each other's burdens.' Not solve them. Not fix them. Not make them go away. Carry them. The image is of two people lifting what one person cannot lift alone. It is not rescue. It is solidarity. That distinction matters enormously, because rescue preserves the hierarchy between helper and helped. Solidarity collapses it. When you carry something heavy alongside someone, you are no longer above them. You are beside them. And that positioning changes everything. Carrying weight together collapses distance. It dissolves roles. When you are holding something heavy with someone else, there is no hierarchy—only humanity. That is what refugees taught me. Not through theory. Not through ideology. But through practice. They stayed when others would have left. They gave when logic said to conserve. They carried when no one else could. And in doing so, they revealed something our culture desperately needs to remember: that community is not proven in moments of celebration, but in moments of strain. I have learned to pay attention to what people do when staying costs them something. Anyone can show up when it is convenient. The question that reveals character is: who stays when it would be reasonable to leave?

Refugees, in my experience, stay. They stay out of a deep understanding that no one makes it alone. They stay because they have been on the receiving end of others' presence in their own darkest hours. They stay because they know what it costs to be left. That knowledge is not abstract. It is embodied. It lives in the body that remembers carrying its mother through a minefield. It lives in the hands that pooled money for a neighbor's rent. It lives in the person who drives an hour to sit in a hospital waiting room for someone they have known for only a year. For readers reflecting on their own lives, the invitation here is not to take on more than you can bear. It is to reconsider how you relate to burden itself. Who knows what you're carrying? Who do you allow to carry with you? Who do you show up for when staying costs something? Shared burden does not require heroics. It begins with presence. With refusing to let people suffer unseen. With choosing proximity over efficiency. Mohammed carried his mother because love demanded it. Years later, he carried others because that was how he understood life to work. The weight was heavy then. It is heavy now. But it is no longer carried alone. And sometimes, that is the truest form of hope we have.

Chapter 8

What They Refused to Lose

The laughter caught me off guard. It didn't feel appropriate—not in the way we're taught to measure moments. The room carried too much history for joy to arrive so easily. Too many stories of loss, displacement, and uncertainty lived quietly in the bodies gathered there. And yet, laughter filled the space. It wasn't polite or restrained. It wasn't the kind that checks to see who might be watching. It rose suddenly, spread quickly, and lingered longer than expected. Someone teased another. Someone else clapped back. A child laughed so hard they lost control of their breath. Music started playing from a phone—nothing formal, nothing planned—and before long, people were moving. This wasn't a celebration because everything had worked out. It was a celebration because life was still here. I had learned, by then, not to underestimate moments like this. Joy among refugees often appears without warning, unannounced, almost defiant.

It does not wait for circumstances to improve. It does not ask permission from grief. It shows up anyway.

CARE Club gatherings were often like this. We would come together for something simple—food, conversation, checking in—and joy would emerge on its own terms. Someone would tell a story. Someone would laugh at themselves. Someone would begin singing. Slowly, the weight of everything people carried loosened just enough for breath to return. What surprised me most was not that joy existed, but how naturally it lived alongside pain. In Western culture, we often separate emotions. We expect grief to look solemn and joy to look carefree. We give each its proper place and time. But among the people I was walking alongside, joy and sorrow shared the same space. They did not cancel each other out. They coexisted. I saw this in celebrations that made no sense on paper. Graduations marked not only achievement, but survival. Birthdays celebrated not just years lived, but years endured. Gatherings happened even when money was tight, even when paperwork remained unresolved, even when family members were still far away. Joy did not mean everything was okay. It meant everything had not been lost. I remember watching people dance who had fled violence. Laugh who had buried loved ones. Celebrate milestones while still carrying unanswered questions about the future. This was not escapism. It was resilience.

Joy, I began to understand, was not the opposite of suffering. It was a refusal to let suffering have the final word. This challenged something deep in me. I had learned to be cautious with joy. To wait until circumstances justified it. To treat celebration as a reward for stability. But refugees did not wait for permission. They celebrated because joy itself was a form of resistance. It said: You did not take everything. It said: We are still human. It said: Life continues. There was courage in that. I saw it when families cooked meals far larger than seemed reasonable, insisting everyone eat. I saw it when music filled rooms that had known silence for too long. I saw it in humor—often sharp, often self-aware—that refused to let despair settle in. This joy was not shallow. It was hard-won. It had passed through grief and survived. It had looked at loss and refused to disappear. There is a theological dimension to this that I have come to take seriously. In the Christian tradition, joy is not described as the absence of suffering—it is described as something that can coexist with suffering. The psalms are full of this paradox. Lament and praise appear sometimes within the same poem, sometimes within the same breath. The psalmist does not resolve the tension between them. He holds it.

That capacity to hold tension—to grieve and celebrate, to mourn and dance, to carry pain and still choose life—is not natural to most of us who have lived lives cushioned by comfort. We expect relief before joy. We expect resolution before celebration. We want the hard part to be over first. Refugees have taught me that this is a luxury, and not a reliable one. Life does not wait for clean endings. Pain and joy intermingle constantly, and the person who refuses to experience joy until all the pain is gone is the person who may wait forever. The gatherings I witnessed were not denial. They were declarations. A declaration that dignity persists. That humanity survives. That the people who tried to break us did not succeed. And in doing so, they taught me something our culture desperately needs to relearn. Joy is not a distraction from reality. It is a declaration that reality is not finished. For readers shaped by a world that often feels heavy—divided, anxious, exhausted—the invitation here is not to force happiness or ignore pain. It is to reconsider what joy is allowed to be. Where have you learned to postpone joy until things improve? Where have you mistaken seriousness for depth? Where have you assumed that laughter means forgetting? Refugees taught me that joy can be an act of memory. A way of remembering who you were before everything broke—and who you still are underneath the scars. Joy does not deny injustice. It does not minimize suffering. It does not rush healing. It creates space to breathe while healing continues. In a world that often feels overwhelmed by bad news and constant urgency, joy reminds us that endurance alone is not enough. We were not meant only to survive. We were meant to live. If immigrants are a gift—and I believe they are—it is because they bring this gift with them. Not naive happiness, but resilient joy. The kind that survives displacement. The kind that rebuilds community. The kind that restores humanity when it feels most fragile. They show us that joy is not something we earn after everything is resolved. Sometimes, joy is what carries us until resolution comes. And sometimes, joy is simply what we refuse to lose.

Chapter 9

Faith Without Fear

They were still waking up when I picked them up. Amari and Yusef shuffled out the door, jackets half-zipped, hair uncombed, carrying the unmistakable energy of boys who had been told it was time to go somewhere before they were ready. They had asked to go to church, though neither of them seemed particularly aware of what kind of Sunday it was. As they got into the car, I said casually, 'Hey guys, do you know what today is?' They shrugged. 'It's Easter,' I said. There was a pause. The kind that tells you people are thinking, not disengaged—searching their memory, turning the question over. Amari spoke first. 'Yeah,' he said slowly, 'that's when we remember when Jesus was born, right?' Before I could respond, Yusef jumped in. 'No, that's Christmas.' I smiled. 'Okay,' I said, 'then you tell him. What's Easter about?'

Yusef went quiet. He stared out the window for a moment, then said, 'Is it something about Jesus dying on a cross?' That was it. No certainty. No performance. Just honesty. As we drove, the conversation unfolded naturally. We talked about Jesus. About what different people believe. About friends who were Muslim. About families who practiced other faiths or none at all. There was no pressure to arrive at the 'right' answer. The questions themselves carried meaning. What struck me most was how unafraid they were to ask. No embarrassment. No anxiety about being wrong. Faith, for them, was not a battlefield—it was a conversation. That posture stayed with me. Not long after, I had another moment that unsettled me in a different way. I picked up a young man who had arrived as a Bhutanese Nepali refugee. He grew up in a Buddhist background and had only recently begun exploring Christianity. Church was still new to him—new language, new rhythms, new assumptions. After the service, as we were walking out, he said, 'I want to come back.' Then he paused, hesitated, and asked a question that stopped me short. 'Is it okay,' he said carefully, 'can Black people come to your church?'

The question was jarring—not because it was malicious, but because it was so honest. It revealed a set of assumptions shaped by history, culture, and experience very different from my own. I didn't hear hostility in his voice. I heard uncertainty. A genuine attempt to understand how faith and community worked in this place he was still learning to navigate. In that moment, I realized something important. Immigrants don't just bring questions about faith. They bring questions that expose our blind spots. They ask things we've learned to avoid saying out loud. They name confusions we've buried beneath politeness or ideology. They reveal how much of what we assume is 'normal' is actually cultural, not theological. For many refugees, pluralism is not theoretical—it's lived. They come from places where religion, ethnicity, and identity have collided violently.

They know what it means to be a minority. They understand difference not as an abstraction, but as a daily reality. When they arrive in a country that promises freedom of religion, they take that promise seriously. They test it. They ask what it really means. Can we worship together even if we don't look alike? Can we disagree and still belong? Can faith be shared without being imposed? These questions are not threats to belief. They are invitations to maturity.

In a polarized culture, faith is often pulled into political camps. Belief becomes a badge of identity rather than a posture of discipleship. Christians learn to defend positions before they learn to listen to people. But Jesus never asked his followers to protect him with fear. He invited them into truth with humility. For followers of Jesus—no matter where you fall politically, no matter how you feel about immigration, borders, or policy—this chapter asks something deeper than agreement. It asks whether our faith is strong enough to be curious. Jesus welcomed questions. He crossed boundaries. He spoke with those outside the religious mainstream. He refused to let fear determine who was worthy of dignity. Faith, as Jesus lived it, was never about dominance. It was about love rooted in truth. This does not mean abandoning conviction. It means anchoring conviction in Christ rather than ideology. You can believe deeply and still listen openly. You can hold to your faith and still honor another's conscience. You can follow Jesus without needing to control the outcomes of every conversation. ——— I have noticed that the most fragile faith is the faith most defended by fear. It requires enemies to survive. It needs a threat to organize around. It mistakes certainty for faithfulness and loudness for courage. But the refugees I have known who carry deep faith—and there are many—do not look like that. Their faith is quieter and somehow more durable. It has been tested by circumstances that would have broken lesser convictions. And it has not broken. It has bent, sometimes. It has asked hard questions. It has sat in silence when answers did not come. But it has not let go. That kind of faith does not need to dominate. It does not need to win every argument. It does not need to protect itself from difficult questions. It can simply be what it is—a steady orientation toward God in the middle of a complicated, uncertain, sometimes painful world. Immigrants reminded me of this—not because they had perfect theology, but because they approached faith with honesty. Their questions were not strategic. They were sincere. And sincerity has a way of cutting through defensiveness. In a world divided by politics, religion, and fear, Christians are called to something better than reaction. We are called to love God and love our neighbor—not selectively, not conditionally, but faithfully. That calling does not change based on who is in power. It does not shift with public opinion. It does not bend to fear. It asks us to examine our hearts before we examine others' beliefs.

For those who want to grow in this posture, the invitation is simple, but not easy. Slow down when questions make you uncomfortable. Listen before correcting. Distinguish between faith and culture. Let love be the loudest witness you offer. Jesus did not tell his followers to win arguments. He told them to follow him. And following him has always meant crossing lines—of fear, of difference, of assumption. Amari and Yusef didn't need a sermon on Easter morning. They needed space to ask. The young man from Bhutan didn't need condemnation. He needed clarity rooted in dignity. In each moment, I was reminded that faith grows best where fear loosens its grip. If immigrants are a gift—and I believe they are—it is because they invite us back to the heart of faith. A faith that is not fragile. A faith that does not need enemies to survive. A faith confident enough to listen, humble enough to learn, and courageous enough to love across difference. That kind of faith doesn't shrink in a pluralistic world. It shines. I want to be honest about something, because I think it matters. The children in the stories above—Amari, Yusef, the young man from Bhutan—were navigating Christian faith, or at least encountering it. But in over ten years of this work, I have walked closely alongside people whose faith looked very different from mine. I have known Muslim families whose devotion to God was so consistent, so unhurried, and so woven into the rhythm of ordinary life that it quietly convicted me. I have known Hindu families whose care for one another, whose patience in suffering, and whose reverence in prayer made me stop and pay attention in a way I did not expect. I am a follower of Jesus. That has not changed. But I would not be honest if I said that witnessing faith in other forms left me unmoved. There was a Muslim father I drove to a job interview early one morning. Before he got out of the car, he paused, faced the window, and prayed quietly. Not for show. Not because I was watching. Simply because that is what he did. His faith was not performed—it was practiced. And something in that moment reached across the distance between us and stirred something in me. There was a Hindu woman I knew who had lost a child in difficult circumstances before resettling here. She carried her grief without bitterness. She lit candles. She brought food to neighbors. She spoke of God—in her own language, in her own way—with a tenderness that I recognized, even if I could not have fully translated it. I did not walk away from those encounters confused about what I believe. I walked away more serious about it. Their faith made me ask whether my own was as lived-in as theirs. Whether I prayed like someone who meant it. Whether my belief showed up in my body and my daily habits, or mostly in the words I used to describe it.

I think that is what genuine faith does, wherever it is found. It asks something of you. It interrupts your comfort. It points beyond yourself. I am not suggesting all faiths lead to the same place. I am saying that God, in his generosity, has allowed me to be taught by people who do not share my tradition—and that I am better for having paid attention. Faith without fear means being secure enough in what you believe to let someone else's devotion challenge you rather than threaten you. It means recognizing that love for God, however it is expressed, is not your enemy. That kind of openness has not weakened my faith. It has deepened it.

Chapter 10

Power That Makes Room

The phone call came late in the evening. My wife had been in the hospital for several days. The kind of days where time stretches and collapses without warning. Where you learn the geography of waiting rooms, memorize the sound of monitors, and live between updates that never feel quite complete. Even when things are stable, they are never settled. You're always bracing for what comes next. When my phone rang, I didn't recognize the number at first. It was Ahmad. He didn't call with advice. He didn't call with a solution. He didn't call to ask for anything. He simply asked how my wife was doing. How we were holding up. Then, quietly, he said, 'If you need anything, please tell me.' I remember ending the call and sitting still for a moment longer than necessary. Because Ahmad had very little. He had arrived as a refugee with fewer resources than I had ever known how to imagine living with.

His life required constant calculation—how to stretch money, how to navigate systems, how to make things work without margin. And yet, in that moment, the direction of care was unmistakable.

He was checking on me. There was something profoundly disarming about that. In my work, I had grown accustomed to being the one who called. The one who checked in. The one who asked what was needed. And here was Ahmad doing the same—not out of obligation or politeness, but out of relationship. It forced me to confront something I hadn't fully named before. Power is not only about what we possess. It is about how we hold it. And sometimes the most formative moments come when the roles quietly reverse—when the one we assume needs help becomes the one who offers it. That phone call stayed with me because it echoed something I had experienced many times before, though I hadn't always recognized it for what it was. Hospitality. Not hospitality as hosting or entertaining, but hospitality as posture. A way of being oriented toward others that doesn't depend on abundance, planning, or control. I had encountered this posture again and again in refugee homes. You walk in, and almost immediately, something is offered. A bottle of water. Tea. Cookies. Whatever is available. Sometimes it's clear there isn't much. Sometimes you know that what's being offered was meant for later.

And yet, it's given freely. You don't need a calendar invite. You don't need to schedule weeks in advance. You don't need to justify your presence. You are simply welcomed. In many of the cultures refugees come from, hospitality is not an event—it is a default. People don't ask whether it's convenient. They ask whether you've eaten. Whether you're okay. Whether you need something. This kind of hospitality does not fit easily into our lives. We are busy. We are scheduled. We are efficient. We protect our time carefully. We manage our availability. We plan connection rather than live into it. And in doing so, we often lose something essential. Connection becomes transactional. Presence becomes conditional. Care becomes delayed, delegated, or outsourced. What refugees taught me—again and again—is that hospitality is not about capacity. It is about orientation. It is not, 'Do I have enough?' It is, 'Who is in front of me?' That realization began to reshape how I understood power itself. In the New Testament, followers of Jesus are instructed to practice hospitality. But the word translated as hospitality carries a depth we often miss. In the original Greek, the word is philoxenia—formed from phileo, meaning love, and xenos, meaning stranger or guest. Literally, it means love of the stranger. Or even more plainly, love of the guest.

Hospitality, in the Christian imagination, was never about hosting friends or welcoming people like us. It was about opening ourselves to those who were unfamiliar, unexpected, and sometimes inconvenient. It was about receiving the other not as a problem to solve, but as a gift to be welcomed. That language changed how I saw everything. Hospitality was not a strategy. It was not a program. It was not even primarily an action. It was a way of seeing. To love the stranger is to resist fear. To welcome the guest is to loosen control. To make room is to trust that God is already present in the encounter. Refugees understood this instinctively. They practiced philoxenia not because it had been explained to them in theological terms, but because life had taught them that dignity and survival depend on mutual care. Hospitality was how community held together when systems failed and certainty disappeared. What humbled me was realizing that many of us who know the word had forgotten its meaning. We had reduced hospitality to something safe and scheduled—something that fit our calendars and comfort levels. But philoxenia is not tidy. It interrupts. It risks. It opens the door before you know what the conversation will require. And yet, it sits at the heart of the Christian faith. Jesus himself lived as a guest—dependent, received, welcomed by those with little to give. And he repeatedly reminded his followers that how we receive the stranger reveals what we believe about God. Seen through that lens, Ahmad's phone call was not unusual. It was faithful. And the countless cups of water, plates of food, and unscheduled welcomes I had experienced were not cultural quirks. They were lived theology. They were power, exercised gently. In America, power often shows up as control—over time, space, resources, outcomes. We value strength that asserts, leadership that directs, efficiency that manages. But the power I saw modeled by refugees was different. It was power that made room. Room for interruption. Room for relationship. Room for mutual care. Ahmad's phone call was not an act of charity. It was an act of dignity. It treated me not as someone above him or responsible for him, but as someone alongside him. That matters. Because the moment we refuse to receive from others, we quietly reinforce hierarchy. We keep ourselves positioned as givers and others as receivers. And in doing so, we miss the possibility of friendship. Refugees did not just accept help from me. They insisted on caring for me too. That insistence changed me. It taught me that true hospitality does not flow in one direction. It circulates. It binds people together through shared attention and shared vulnerability. I began to see how often power becomes harsh simply because it does not know how to be gentle. How authority grows loud when it is insecure. How control tightens when trust is absent. But what I witnessed in refugee communities was authority expressed through restraint. Care offered without condition. Presence given without agenda. This did not mean boundaries disappeared. Life was still complex. Time was still limited. But underneath it all was a shared assumption: we belong to one another. And belonging changes how power is used. It asks leaders to listen before acting. It invites strength to serve rather than dominate. It allows generosity to exist even in scarcity. In a society driven by productivity and performance, hospitality feels inefficient. It interrupts. It slows us down. It asks us to be available rather than impressive. But that interruption is precisely the point. For readers reflecting on their own lives, the invitation here is not to abandon responsibility or structure. It is to ask a deeper question: How do I hold the power I've been given? Do I use it to protect myself from inconvenience? Do I guard it so carefully that others cannot approach? Or do I allow it to make room—for people, for presence, for mutual care? Hospitality is not about being constantly open. It is about being genuinely open when it matters. Power used gently creates spaces where trust can grow. Where people feel safe enough to offer help back. Where dignity is preserved on both sides of the relationship. Ahmad did not know if I needed anything. He simply wanted me to know that I was not carrying it alone. That is the kind of power that heals. If immigrants are a gift—and I believe they are—it is because they remind us of this quieter strength. A strength that does not announce itself. A hospitality that does not require abundance. An authority that serves rather than controls. In a culture obsessed with leverage and influence, they invite us back to something older and truer: Showing up. Making room. Loving the guest. ——— That kind of power does not dominate. It dignifies.

Chapter 11

When Faith Is All You Have

The email came from a familiar name. Stephanie and I had spent a summer together years earlier with an organization on the east side of Indonesia when I was still in high school. We had stayed in touch in the loose but meaningful way people do when shared experiences have shaped them deeply. Over time, our lives had gone in different directions, but the connection remained. Her message carried an excitement that was hard to miss. She explained that her son had spent time in Nairobi, Kenya, years earlier, living in the home of a pastor there. That pastor, she wrote, was a refugee from the Congo. And now—through the refugee resettlement program—he had been accepted to come to the United States. 'He's settling in Indianapolis,' she said. 'Would you be willing to meet him?' When I looked up the address she sent, I realized he lived less than twenty minutes from me. That's how I met Patrick. Patrick had been in America for about three years when we first sat down together. His English was limited at the time, and conversation moved slowly. But his presence was unmistakable—focused, steady, attentive. He carried himself like someone who had learned how to endure.

Patrick had not finished high school before coming to the United States. Within months of arriving, he earned his GED. He committed himself to learning English. He enrolled in a local Bible school and began continuing his education with discipline and joy. Slowly, deliberately, he built a life. But what struck me most was not his progress. It was his devotion. Patrick is a gifted leader. He travels extensively across the United States, speaking and teaching among networks of refugee churches, particularly within the Banyamulenge community of the Congo—a people who have endured genocide, displacement, and generations of oppression. Many families from his tribe have been resettled throughout America, carrying trauma that does not dissolve simply because a border has been crossed. Every time we talk, Patrick returns to his people. He speaks of injustice in Africa not with bitterness, but with responsibility. He prays for those still suffering. He organizes, encourages, and shepherds communities scattered far from home. Leadership, for him, is not a platform—it is a burden he willingly carries. Together, we helped start a church for refugee families in our city. It is not large. It does not have much money. It does not resemble the churches many Americans are used to. But it is alive. ———

What I witnessed there unsettled me—in the best possible way. Faith, in that space, was not theoretical. Worship was not casual. Prayer was not symbolic. God was not discussed as an idea, but relied upon as a presence. Faith was not one part of life. It was the thing holding everything else together. Patrick's faith had been tested by violence, displacement, and loss. What remained was not anger or despair, but clarity. Faith did not make his life easier. It made it possible. I saw the same clarity in a Spanish-speaking church I visited not long after. The room was modest but full. There were people from more than ten countries gathered together—many immigrants, some refugees, all navigating life in a country that often felt unfamiliar and uncertain. Political tensions loomed outside the walls. Immigration policies shifted. Futures remained unresolved. And yet, inside that space, there was no anxiety. There was singing—unpolished and wholehearted. There was prayer—direct, expectant, unguarded. There was trust—not naive, but practiced. What struck me most was the absence of distraction. No one was curating an image. No one was posturing. No one was hedging belief. Faith was not competing with a dozen other loyalties. It was central. As I sat there, I realized that every refugee church I had visited shared something else in common. They were all made up of Black and brown bodies. Congolese. Central American. East African. South Asian. Caribbean. Middle Eastern. People whose skin, accents, and histories marked them immediately as racial minorities in America. Many of them arrived from places where they had already been minorities—because of tribe, ethnicity, or religion. But few arrived with a full understanding of America's racial history. They did not come shaped by the long shadow of slavery, Jim Crow laws, redlining, and segregation. They did not carry the same inherited narratives of race that dominate American life. They arrived simply as themselves. Over time, of course, they would learn. They would experience suspicion, misrecognition, and exclusion. They would discover that Black and brown bodies are read differently here. That freedom is real but uneven. That opportunity exists, but not equally. And yet, their faith did not begin with American categories. They worshiped without first asking where they fit in the racial hierarchy. They prayed without calculating social advantage. Their devotion was unselfconscious, sincere, unprotected by cultural power. Faith, for them, was not reinforced by dominance. It was refined by dependence. What I was witnessing in these churches was not intensity for its own sake. It was attentiveness. Faith had not been crowded out by excess. It had not been diluted by constant choice. It had not been forced to compete with a thousand other allegiances. There was room for God. In refugee churches, faith is rarely abstract. It is not something discussed primarily in terms of opinion or preference. It is something practiced because it must be. Prayer is not ornamental. Worship is not background noise. Scripture is not symbolic—it is direction. This kind of faith does not rush. It waits. It listens. It trusts slowly and deeply. I noticed how often refugee Christians spoke about God in ways that assumed God's nearness rather than God's approval. They were not trying to prove belief or defend correctness. They were trying to remain faithful—to stay aligned with what they believed was good, true, and sustaining. That posture felt increasingly rare to me. American Christians are not lacking faith. But we are often distracted. Our spiritual lives compete with political power, financial security, retirement plans, markets, possessions, and the constant pull of influence. Faith becomes one voice among many. God becomes something we fit in rather than center our lives around. Refugee Christians rarely have that luxury. When you have lost your home, your safety, and your certainty, faith is no longer an accessory. It becomes a lifeline. This is not to romanticize suffering. No one I met wished for what they had endured. But there is a clarity that emerges when everything else is stripped away. Faith becomes simple—not simplistic, but focused. It sustains. It guides. It brings hope without guarantees. Patrick did not speak of God as an abstract belief. He spoke as someone who had relied on God when there were no backups, no safety nets, no illusions of control. And that kind of faith is confronting. Not because it condemns us, but because it reveals us. It reveals how easily we confuse comfort with blessing. How quickly we equate faithfulness with stability. How tempted we are to measure God's goodness by outcomes rather than presence. Refugee churches quietly challenge all of that. They remind us that faith was never meant to secure power. It was meant to anchor hope. It was never meant to guarantee comfort. It was meant to sustain love. This is not a call for American Christians to abandon engagement in the world. It is a call to examine what we have allowed to compete with our devotion. What remains of faith when influence fades? What holds us when money cannot protect us? What anchors us when certainty disappears? For many refugee Christians, these are not philosophical questions. They are lived realities. And still, faith endures. Not loud. Not angry. Not performative. Faith that has been tested tends to grow quieter, deeper, steadier. When faith is all you have, it becomes enough.

This chapter is not a rebuke. It is an invitation. An invitation to simplicity. To humility. To learning from those whose faith has survived what ours has often been shielded from. Patrick did not come to America to teach us a lesson. But through his devotion, his kindness, and his steady leadership, he has done exactly that. He has reminded me that faith does not need constant reinforcement from power, wealth, or certainty. It needs trust. It needs dependence. It needs the courage to believe when belief is costly. If immigrants are a gift—and I believe they are—it is because they help us recover what we are in danger of losing. A faith that does not cling to control. A faith that does not fear scarcity. A faith that endures when faith is all you have. And that kind of faith still has the power to change us.

Chapter 12

Where Leadership Begins

We called it Champions. It was a three-month initiative for young immigrant kids—many of them navigating life in a new country while carrying responsibilities far beyond their years. The goal was simple but intentional: to help them see themselves rightly. We made t-shirts that said, I am a leader. Not because they had positions or titles. Not because they were in charge of anything. But because leadership begins long before anyone gives you authority. It begins with how you lead yourself. One day, during a session, I asked the group a question. 'What is a leader?' The room was alive with energy—kids talking, moving, laughing, half-listening, half-processing. And then, without hesitation, a first grader spoke up. He had been running around moments earlier—full of life, restless, brilliant. He had come from Africa not long before. 'A leader,' he said, 'is someone with resilience.' The room went quiet. I was stunned—not just that he answered so quickly, but what he said. That word doesn't usually come from first graders. It comes from people who have learned, early on, that life will test you. That things will not go the way you want. That you will have to keep going anyway. 'That's exactly right,' I told him. And in that moment, I realized he hadn't been taught that definition in a classroom. He had learned it by living. Most of us spend our energy trying to control outcomes and manage opinions. We try to shape how we are seen or remembered. And when these things don't move the way we want, we feel frustrated, defeated, or lost. But those who make the greatest impact are not the ones who control their world. They are the ones who are able to see and live differently. They still endure chaos, opposition, and uncertainty—but they do not begin by trying to master everything around them. They begin by mastering themselves. This is where leadership should begin. Refugees understand this intuitively. Leadership, for them, is not about influence or image. It is about endurance. Responsibility. Making the next faithful decision when the future is unclear. Many of the young people we walked alongside were already leading—translating for parents, navigating systems, caring for siblings, choosing integrity in environments that offered easier shortcuts. No one applauded them. No one gave them a title. But they were becoming leaders anyway. What they taught me is that leadership is not primarily about what you do. It is about who you are becoming.

In American culture, leadership is often framed as visibility, platform, or power. We talk about influence, reach, and control. We measure success by outcomes and recognition. But that definition rarely produces resilient people. It produces anxious ones. Because when leadership is built on control, it collapses the moment control is lost. Refugee leadership looks different. It begins internally. It grows quietly. It is shaped by restraint more than assertion. And it aligns deeply with the Christian vision of leadership. In the Christian tradition, leadership does not begin with self-assertion. It begins with surrender. Jesus did not model leadership by grasping power, but by relinquishing it. He did not call people to dominate, but to follow. And following him has always required a shift—from willfulness to willingness. That distinction matters. Willfulness says, I will make this happen. Willingness says, I will be shaped by what is true. This is why leadership formation in Christianity has always been spiritual before it is strategic. It is not about trying harder. It is about learning to yield—to wisdom, to guidance, to a strength beyond your own. This is something people in recovery understand deeply. In 12-step programs, the first movements are not about self-mastery through control. They are about admitting limitation, naming dependence, and turning toward a Higher Power. Healing begins not when someone tightens their grip, but when they loosen it. Christian leadership works the same way. We do not become better leaders by sheer willpower. We become better leaders by becoming more honest, more humble, more open to being formed. This kind of leadership grows from surrender—not passivity, but trust. A trust that God's strength can meet us where ours runs thin. That wisdom is given, not manufactured. That character matters more than control. And the fruit of this kind of leadership is not domination or success at any cost. It looks like love. Joy that isn't dependent on outcomes. Peace that steadies others. Patience under pressure. Kindness that disarms fear. Gentleness that does not need to prove itself. Self-control that resists impulse and ego. These are not soft qualities. They are resilient ones. ——— I have watched refugee young people exercise this kind of leadership in ways that I have rarely seen modeled in boardrooms or pulpits. I have watched a seventeen-year-old girl sit with her grieving mother and translate not just words, but emotions—holding two worlds together so her family could survive a crisis. I have watched a young man choose honesty in a moment when lying would have been easy, because his integrity meant more to him than his comfort.

These were not remarkable acts by remarkable people. They were ordinary acts by people who had been formed by hardship into something durable. The first grader who answered my question had not studied leadership theory. He had practiced it. He had been formed by a life that required resilience before he could even spell the word. That formation is not something we can program or shortcut. It grows in the soil of genuine difficulty—of being tested and choosing, again and again, to keep going rather than collapse. But we can create conditions for it. We can build spaces where young people are trusted with real responsibility. Where failure is treated as formation rather than verdict. Where integrity is noticed and named. Where the quiet acts of faithfulness are seen as more important than the visible acts of performance. If you are leading—yourself, your family, a classroom, a church, an organization—this is where the work begins. Not with a platform. Not with a strategy. Not with recognition. But with attention. With learning to pause instead of react. With choosing integrity when no one is watching. With asking what kind of person your leadership is forming. Refugee children reminded me of this. They did not talk about leadership as something you gain. They spoke of it as something you practice—daily, imperfectly, courageously.

A first grader knew that resilience mattered because he had needed it. That is the kind of leader our world needs. Not louder voices. Not tighter control. But people who have learned to lead themselves with humility, courage, and surrender. Leadership does not begin when you are given authority. It begins when you learn who you are willing to become. And that kind of leadership—quiet, resilient, rooted—has the power to shape families, communities, and futures long after the applause fades.

Chapter 13

Becoming Human Together

One of the things I've told my two grown children over the years is simple, but not easy to live out. Continue to be you—because everyone else is already taken. It's the kind of line that sounds like a cliché until you realize how much of life is spent trying to become someone else. Trying to fit an image. Trying to belong by blending in. Trying to succeed by imitating whatever version of 'normal' happens to be rewarded in the moment. But becoming fully human has never been about becoming like everyone else. It has always been about becoming who we were created to be. That truth has been reinforced in me, again and again, through relationships with immigrants and refugees. People whose lives, cultures, histories, and assumptions are profoundly different from mine—and yet whose humanity is unmistakably shared. Every conversation has carried this quiet reminder: everyone has something to offer the world. Not in the abstract. Not someday. But now—formed by their uniqueness, their story, their losses, their resilience, and their hope.

Refugees did not arrive as blank slates. They arrived as whole people. They brought memories of home countries I had never seen. Ways of raising children that challenged my assumptions. Understandings of community that felt foreign to my individualism. Faith shaped by suffering. Humor sharpened by survival.

Hospitality practiced without abundance. And slowly, often without realizing it, I found myself changing. Not becoming less myself—but becoming more human. We are often told that difference is something to manage. Something to tolerate. Something to overcome in order to get along. But what I learned is that difference is not the problem. Disconnection is. When difference is held at a distance, it becomes threatening. When it is encountered through relationship, it becomes enriching. We begin to see that similarity alone does not create depth. It is difference—held with curiosity and respect—that stretches us. Refugees taught me that becoming human together requires humility. It requires admitting that my way is not the only way. That my upbringing, my culture, my assumptions are not universal. That I am shaped by forces I did not choose—and so is everyone else. This is not about erasing identity. It is about honoring it.

When we recognize that each person carries a unique story, shaped by history, culture, trauma, and joy, something softens in us. Judgment gives way to understanding. Fear loosens its grip. We begin to listen not to respond, but to learn. I saw this in small, ordinary moments. In conversations where language was limited, but meaning was shared. In disagreements that didn't fracture relationship. In laughter that crossed cultures. In faith practiced differently, but sincerely. ——— These moments reminded me that unity is not sameness. It is mutual recognition. We become better people when we allow others to remain fully themselves—when we resist the urge to flatten difference or demand conformity. And we become wiser when we let those differences teach us. Refugees did not ask me to abandon who I am. They invited me to examine it. Why do I value what I value? Why do I fear what I fear? Why do I assume my experience is the norm? Those questions are uncomfortable. But they are formative. I think about the particular kind of examination that happens when your assumptions are challenged not by argument but by relationship. It is much harder to dismiss a point of view when it is attached to a person you know. When that person has sat at your table. When you have driven them somewhere important. When you have watched them navigate something you could not navigate yourself. The arguments we have in the abstract—about immigration, about belonging, about who counts as a neighbor—tend to flatten people into positions. But the people I have come to know resisted that flattening every time I tried to apply it. They were always more complex, more surprising, more fully human than any category could contain. That is one of the great gifts of genuine relationship across difference. It makes ideology harder to sustain. Not because ideas don't matter—they do—but because people are always more than their representative function. Becoming human together does not mean agreement on everything. It means commitment to one another's dignity.

It means choosing relationship over reduction. It means believing that no culture, no nation, no person holds the full picture alone. This chapter is not a call to sentimentality. It is a call to maturity. Mature humanity recognizes complexity. It holds difference without panic. It stays curious when easy narratives fall apart. It refuses to divide the world into heroes and villains. Refugees taught me this not because they were trying to teach, but because they lived it. Their lives required adaptation. Their survival depended on relationship. Their hope was sustained through community. They became who they were through connection—not isolation. And so do we. In a world that constantly pressures us to choose sides, to harden identities, to retreat into echo chambers, becoming human together is a quiet act of resistance. It insists that our differences are not liabilities, but gifts. That our shared humanity is deeper than our divisions. The lesson my children learned early—the lesson refugees reinforced in me—is this: You do not become more human by becoming someone else. You become more human by becoming more fully yourself—and making room for others to do the same. That is how communities are formed. That is how trust is built. That is how hope takes root. We do not lose ourselves in relationship. We find ourselves there. And when we do, something extraordinary happens. We begin—slowly, imperfectly, courageously—to become human together.

Chapter 14

The Hands That Sewed Hope

When the world first began shutting down during COVID, confusion spread almost as quickly as the virus itself. No one seemed to know exactly what was happening. Grocery store shelves emptied. Schools closed. Churches stopped gathering. News reports became daily counts of infection rates, hospitalizations, and deaths.

Every conversation carried uncertainty. Every cough carried suspicion. At first, there were no political arguments about masks where we lived. That came later. In those early weeks, people were simply afraid. People were dying. One of the first deaths that shook our community happened at my son's high school — the second largest high school in our state. The head of the athletic department died from the virus. Suddenly COVID was no longer something happening somewhere else. It was here. Personal. Close enough to touch our own families. Fear settled over the city like a fog. And then another problem emerged. There were not enough masks.

Hospitals struggled to get them. Nursing homes needed them. Shelters needed them. Ordinary families could not find them in stores. Supply chains broke down almost overnight. Something as simple as fabric over a face suddenly became precious. I remember sitting with the growing realization that many of the refugee families we knew possessed something the wider community suddenly needed. Hands. Skilled hands. Many of the women we served knew how to make things. Sewing, stitching, repairing, creating — these were not hobbies for many of them. These were survival skills carried across oceans and refugee camps and years of rebuilding life in unfamiliar places. And so a small idea began to emerge. What if we made masks ourselves? At first, it sounded almost impossible. Many families did not even own sewing machines. Others had never used one before. Some had the desire to help but lacked confidence. Everyone was still navigating fear, uncertainty, and isolation. But something beautiful happens when people are given the opportunity to contribute rather than merely receive. Hope begins to move. We started gathering sewing machines. Donations arrived from different places. Tables became workspaces. Fabric appeared in stacks and bundles. Thread, elastic, scissors, patterns — ordinary objects suddenly became tools of compassion. Two twin sisters from the Mon tribe of Myanmar came to help lead the effort. Their family had resettled in northern Indiana years earlier, and the sisters had recently graduated from college. They carried both gentleness and quiet strength about them. Patiently, they began teaching families and individuals how to use sewing machines. Some people had never sewn before. The sisters would lean over shoulders, guiding hands carefully through the rhythm of the machine. Foot pedal. Needle. Thread. Fold. Stitch. Start again. Little by little, uncertainty turned into purpose. The sound of sewing machines filled rooms where anxiety had once dominated conversation. At the same time, another quiet movement of service was happening throughout the apartment community itself. Young people began helping disinfect shared spaces. They wiped down door handles, railings, laundry rooms, entryways, staircases, and common areas. Every day brought new fears about how the virus spread, and many families lived in close proximity to one another. Shared spaces suddenly carried anxiety. But instead of retreating entirely into fear, many of the youth stepped forward to help protect their neighbors.

Buckets of disinfectant and paper towels became instruments of care. Teenagers moved through hallways wiping surfaces that most people normally ignored. Apartment doors opened and closed throughout the day while young volunteers quietly worked to help elderly residents, vulnerable families, and frightened neighbors feel a little safer. No cameras followed them. No media outlets told their stories. No one called them heroes. But they were serving their community all the same. I often think about how easy it is for societies to define refugees only by what they lack. They need housing. They need jobs. They need language classes. They need transportation. They need support. And all of that is true. But beneath those needs are also gifts, skills, resilience, creativity, courage, and compassion waiting to be seen. Too often we only ask, We rarely ask, During COVID, I watched refugees become protectors of the city around them.

Not through speeches. Not through power. Not through recognition. But through quiet service. Mask after mask was sewn by hands that knew hardship intimately. Many of these families had already lived through war, displacement, uncertainty, and loss long before the pandemic arrived in America. Perhaps suffering had taught them something the rest of us were only beginning to learn — that fragile moments require communities to hold one another together. In many ways, the refugee families understood collective survival better than most Americans did. They already knew what it meant to rely on neighbors. They knew how quickly life could change. They knew uncertainty. They knew adaptation. They knew how fragile stability could be. And maybe that is why they responded not only with fear, but with action. In the end, we estimated that nearly 1,500 masks were made and distributed. Some went to families. Some went to vulnerable members of the community.

Some went to homeless shelters at a time when supplies were still painfully limited. I still remember bringing boxes of masks to shelters and organizations serving those without homes. Before masks became easy to purchase online or available in every store, these simple pieces of fabric carried real significance. They represented protection. Care. Presence. Someone thinking about another human being. And no one asked whether the recipients deserved them. That is one of the things love does. Love does not always pause to calculate worthiness before responding to need. It simply moves toward vulnerability. What struck me most was not merely the number of masks produced, but the spirit in which they were made. There was laughter in some of those rooms. Conversation. Shared meals. Imperfect stitching. Frustration. Learning. Quiet pride. Children carried stacks of finished masks across rooms. Parents worked late into the evening. Young adults translated instructions between languages. Neighbors checked on elderly residents. People who had once arrived in America needing help were now helping hold together the wider community around them. In the middle of global fear, people were still creating something together.

The pandemic revealed many fractures in society. Fear isolated people from one another. Suspicion spread quickly. Differences hardened. Eventually even masks themselves became symbols in cultural arguments. But before all of that polarization took hold, I witnessed something else first. Human beings caring for one another. Refugees sewing masks for strangers. Immigrant families protecting homeless neighbors. Young people disinfecting hallways to protect the elderly. Twin sisters teaching practical skills with patience and dignity. Communities rediscovering interdependence. The kingdom of God rarely arrives with spectacle. More often it sounds like the hum of sewing machines in a small room while ordinary people quietly love their neighbors. Or the sound of disinfectant bottles spraying door handles in apartment hallways while teenagers choose responsibility over indifference. COVID taught me many things, but one lesson continues to stay with me: People flourish when they are invited to contribute, not merely survive.

Hospitality is incomplete if it only creates receivers. True belonging creates participation. Dignity deepens when people know they are needed. One of the quiet tragedies of modern society is how often vulnerable people are viewed primarily through deficiency. We measure what they lack before we recognize what they carry. But every person longs for more than survival. People long to matter. To create. To protect. To serve. To belong. To know their presence has value. I saw that longing come alive during those months. I saw refugees become neighbors. I saw young people become caretakers. I saw service become healing. I saw fear interrupted by purpose. And perhaps that is one of the hidden mysteries of compassion: when we help others carry burdens, we often rediscover our own humanity in the process. The guests became givers. And in many ways, they always were.

Chapter 15

The Gift of the Table

After years of traveling and living overseas, I had grown accustomed to a very different understanding of hospitality than what many Americans experience. In much of the world, you do not always need a formal invitation to visit someone's home. You simply go. You stop by. You knock on the door. You enter into life already happening. And almost always, food appears. Tea appears first in many places. Then bread. Rice. Soup. Fruit. Whatever the family has. Hospitality in much of the world is not treated as a carefully scheduled event. It is woven into ordinary life itself. That sometimes surprised new volunteers working with refugee families. Many Americans are deeply shaped by time-driven culture. We schedule lunches two weeks ahead. We apologize for stopping by unexpectedly. We worry whether the house is clean enough, whether there is enough food, whether the timing is inconvenient.

But much of the world operates more relationally than chronologically. The event matters more than the clock. People linger. Conversations stretch. Meals unfold slowly. Guests are folded into the rhythm of daily life rather than inserted into empty calendar spaces. I would often have volunteers ask, "When is a good time for us to visit?" And sometimes the answer was simply: "Just go." Not because planning is wrong, but because many refugee families did not experience hospitality as performance. Hospitality was presence. I remember walking into Abdul's apartment one evening after a long day. Before I even reached the door, I could already smell onions, garlic, and spices drifting into the hallway. Children moved in and out of rooms. Voices overlapped. The television hummed softly in the background while pots simmered somewhere in the kitchen. The apartment was alive. As soon as I stepped inside, Abdul smiled broadly and motioned for me to sit. And almost immediately, the familiar ritual began. I laughed because I already knew resistance was pointless.

Years overseas had taught me that in many cultures, refusing food too quickly can unintentionally communicate distance. The meal itself is rarely just about hunger. The meal says: You are welcome. You belong here. We are honored by your presence. Within minutes plates appeared from every direction. Rice. Flatbread. Chicken. Tea poured into small glasses. And somehow, no matter how limited a family's resources were, there was always enough to share. That always moved me deeply because many of the families preparing these meals had themselves experienced profound scarcity. Some had lived in refugee camps. Some had fled war. Some had lost homes, careers, extended family members, and entire ways of life. Yet generosity still flowed from them almost instinctively. Not generosity from abundance of possessions. Generosity from abundance of heart. There is a woman I will call Fatima — a Somali grandmother who had been in the United States for several years when I first visited her home. She had raised children across three countries. She had buried a husband. She had navigated bureaucracies in languages she did not speak and rebuilt a life in a city that did not always feel like it wanted her there.

Her apartment was small. Her furniture was sparse. Her kitchen was modest by almost any measure. But when I arrived at her door, the table was already set. I had not been expected. I had simply come by to check on a family matter — a form that needed signing, a question about a school enrollment. Practical business. The kind of visit that takes fifteen minutes. But Fatima would not hear of it. She sat me down, disappeared into the kitchen, and returned with tea, bread, and a bowl of suuqaar — a Somali dish of seasoned meat and vegetables that smelled like something between a stew and a celebration. I tried to explain that I had only stopped for a moment. That I did not want to trouble her. She looked at me with an expression I have come to recognize over the years — the look that says your refusal is not only unnecessary, it is slightly absurd. I stayed for two hours. We talked about her grandchildren, about her neighborhood, about the small garden she was trying to grow on her balcony. She asked about my family. I told her about my kids. We laughed more than I expected to. When I finally stood to leave, she packed the remaining bread into a bag and pressed it into my hands. She would not let me walk out empty.

There is something in that gesture that I have never forgotten — the insistence that a guest not leave without being nourished. It is a theology of generosity I have rarely seen practiced so consistently or so naturally. Another memory stays with me from a community dinner we organized one year — an event we called Neighbors at the Table. The idea was simple: bring refugee families and long-term residents of the city together for a shared meal, each family contributing a dish from their own tradition. What arrived that evening was extraordinary. Tables filled with food I could barely name. Injera from Ethiopia. Jollof rice from West Africa. Steamed dumplings from Myanmar. A fragrant lamb dish from Afghanistan. Sweet fried plantains. Mango salad. Homemade flatbreads of every variety. Desserts that tasted like the memory of somewhere far away. People stood around the food before the meal began, asking questions and listening to the answers. Where does this come from? What is in this? How do you make it? And something happened in those exchanges that no panel discussion or community meeting had ever quite produced. People became curious about each other. Not as categories. Not as cases. Not as the kind of conversation where someone asks questions already loaded with assumptions.

Just genuine human curiosity — the kind that says, tell me about your world. Show me what you love. Let me taste what your mother made. A woman named Miriam —

a longtime resident of the neighborhood who had initially been skeptical about the event — spent forty-five minutes talking to a young mother from Congo about a dish made with cassava leaves. By the end of the evening they had exchanged phone numbers. They had plans to cook together the following week. I do not know if that friendship lasted. I hope it did. But what I know is that the table created an opening that no other format could have made. Food is disarming in a way that arguments never are. You cannot easily fear someone who has fed you. You cannot hold a stranger at arm's length when their hands have passed you bread. I have thought often about why table hospitality carries such particular power — why sitting down to eat together seems to soften things that nothing else quite reaches. Part of it is physical. Eating is one of the most human things we do. It is intimate and ordinary at the same time. Around a table, status tends to flatten. The person who arrived with credentials and the person who arrived with nothing both need to eat. Both reach for the same bread. Part of it is attention. A meal requires presence. It is very difficult to be fully distracted while someone is filling your plate and watching your face to see if you enjoy what they have made for you. And part of it, I think, is simply that cooking for someone is one of the most direct expressions of care that exists. It says, I thought about you before you arrived. I prepared something for you. I wanted you to feel full when you left. That is love made edible. The families we served taught me this not through lectures or explanations, but through practice. They simply kept setting the table. They kept pouring the tea. They kept sending me home with leftovers I had not asked for and could not refuse. And slowly, over years of being welcomed in this way, I found that my own hospitality began to change. I became less worried about whether the timing was right, whether the house was clean, whether there was enough. I started to understand that the people coming through my door were not inconveniences to be managed. They were gifts. And gifts deserve a table.

Chapter 16

When Children Lead

I first met James at one of our weekly gatherings not long after his family arrived in America. He was quiet. Not withdrawn in an unhealthy way, but observant — the kind of quiet that watches a room carefully before speaking. He was young, unsure of his English, and still adjusting to an entirely new world. When he told me he was from Malawi, I smiled immediately. Years earlier, as a student, I had spent time in Malawi myself. I still remembered a little Chichewa, and so I greeted him with a few words from his language. His face changed instantly. It was small — just a smile, really — but it was the kind of smile that appears when someone suddenly realizes they are not completely invisible. James' story, like many refugee stories, was more layered than people often assume. His family had fled the violence and instability of Burundi years earlier and eventually found refuge in Malawi, where he spent much of his childhood before later being resettled to America through the U.S. refugee program. By the time I met him, he had already crossed multiple worlds before even reaching high school. And yet there he sat quietly in our community gathering — trying to learn a new language, navigate a new culture, and build a new future once again. That is one of the things many Americans do not fully realize about refugee children. When they arrive, they are not merely learning words.

They are learning an entire world — how schools function, how friendships form, how humor works, how teachers speak, how to navigate social expectations that most American children absorb without ever thinking about them. And while children are doing all of that adapting, their parents are often carrying enormous burdens of their own. Jobs, rent, bills, transportation, healthcare, paperwork, language barriers, trauma, exhaustion. Some work long factory shifts while still learning basic English. Others carry the emotional weight of war, displacement, or years spent in refugee camps before ever arriving in America. Children often absorb all of this silently. And yet they also adapt with remarkable resilience. I sensed something special in James early on. He was thoughtful, steady, curious. Even while struggling with language, there was something quietly determined about him. He did not demand attention. He simply kept showing up. Listening. Learning. Growing. Over the years, it became beautiful to watch his life unfold. The teenager who once sat quietly in unfamiliar rooms slowly became confident. School became less intimidating. Friendships formed. Opportunities opened. Eventually James graduated from high school, went on to college, and later pursued graduate studies while building a meaningful career. I remembered the beginning. I remembered the uncertainty, the quietness, the long process of becoming. And the distance between those two moments — the boy sitting silently in our gathering and the man he grew into

— still fills me with something close to awe. I watched similar transformations happen many times. Young refugees becoming nurses, teachers, counselors, business owners, interpreters, engineers, social workers, and community leaders. Children who once felt invisible slowly discovering confidence and voice. But not every story unfolds beautifully, and that is important to say honestly. Refugee youth often carry pressures many people never see. The pressure to succeed. The pressure to help their families survive. The pressure of navigating two cultures simultaneously. Some feel they belong nowhere fully — too American for their parents' culture, too foreign for America. Living between worlds can become exhausting, especially for teenagers trying to discover who they are while also carrying the expectations and anxieties of entire families. No child's future is guaranteed simply because opportunity exists nearby. Children still need guidance, stability, encouragement, community, and adults who genuinely see them. I remember one young man — I will call him Elias — who arrived from East Africa in his early teens. Bright, charismatic, with a laugh that filled whatever room he was in. For two years he thrived. Then high school hit harder than expected. An older peer group pulled at him. Grades slipped. He started disappearing from programs and gatherings where he had once been a regular presence. One of our long-term volunteers, a man named David who had mentored youth for years, simply refused to stop showing up for Elias. He kept calling. Kept stopping by. Kept inviting him for coffee, for lunch, for car rides to nowhere in particular. No speeches. No conditions. Just steady, patient presence. It took the better part of a year. But slowly Elias came back. Not all at once — gradually, the way trust rebuilds after it has been strained. He finished school. He found work. He eventually told David that those calls during his worst months were the only thing that had reminded him anyone still believed in him. Belonging grows through repeated human presence, not programs alone. That is true for every child, but it is especially true for children carrying the weight of two worlds. One of the beautiful surprises of this work was discovering how naturally children move toward one another across difference.

Adults often enter multicultural spaces cautiously. We worry about saying the wrong thing. We carry assumptions, politics, stereotypes, and anxieties into the room before relationships even begin. Children usually begin somewhere much simpler. That is often enough. I watched American children and refugee children become friends despite sharing almost no common language. A soccer ball could accomplish what formal meetings sometimes could not.

A basketball game dissolved awkwardness faster than carefully planned icebreakers. I remember one Saturday afternoon during an outdoor event when a group of Somali boys and a group of American kids from a visiting volunteer group ended up on opposite sides of a makeshift soccer field. Within twenty minutes, the teams had reshuffled entirely. Kids were playing together, yelling in fragments of each other's languages, celebrating goals with the same leaping enthusiasm regardless of who scored. Afterward I watched a Somali boy named Hassan — who had been in America for less than three months — teaching a red-haired American kid how to count to ten in Somali, laughing every time the pronunciation went sideways. The American kid was practicing the same ten words on a loop, delighted each time Hassan confirmed he had finally gotten one right.

Neither seemed frustrated by the barriers between them. They just kept trying. Children often possess a flexibility adults lose. They have not yet fully learned the habit of fearing difference. Adults often begin with categories — where are you from, what do you believe, are you like me. Children more often begin with participation — can you play, do you want to join us, can you come too. That simplicity carries more wisdom than we usually credit it with. I think often about how Jesus consistently placed children near the center of His vision of the kingdom of God. Not because children are morally perfect, but perhaps because children often remain open in ways adults become guarded. Open to wonder. Open to trust. Open to receiving people without immediately categorizing them. Adults become experts at self-protection. Children still risk connection. Much of what shapes a child's heart is quietly modeled long before it is formally taught. Children watch adults constantly. They notice not merely what we say, but how we respond to people who are different from us. They learn fear or openness from us. Compassion or suspicion. Generosity or hospitality. Children are rarely born fearing people they do not understand. Much of that fear is learned. But so is kindness. So is curiosity. So is welcome.

And perhaps part of raising healthy children — whether our own or the ones we encounter through this kind of work — is not merely preparing them to succeed in the world, but helping them remain human within it. Tender without becoming weak. Compassionate without becoming naive. Open without losing wisdom. I still think about James sometimes. About the young teenager who once sat quietly in a room full of unfamiliar people and unfamiliar language. I wonder how many people looked at him then and saw only limitation. But hidden inside that quiet teenager was enormous possibility waiting for room to grow. That is true for so many children. A child translating for a parent today may become a leader tomorrow. A shy teenager struggling through English homework today may someday help others navigate their own transitions. A young refugee trying to belong today may someday create belonging for countless others. Children are never merely the future. They are already shaping the world around them now. Often more beautifully than adults realize. And sometimes, if we pay close enough attention, they become our teachers too.

Chapter 17

Thinking in Decades and Generations

Thinking in Decades and Generations One of the things I often tell refugee students is this: Every American has a migration story. Sometimes they look surprised when I say that. Perhaps it is because many immigrants and refugees grow up feeling as though they alone are the newcomers, while everyone else somehow belongs naturally to the land around them. But America itself is a story of movement, migration, risk, struggle, survival, and rebuilding. Even my own family carries such a story. I sometimes tell students about two Vestals who crossed the ocean generations ago on a ship coming to America. One of them died during the journey and was buried at sea before ever reaching the shores of the country they hoped would become home. When I tell that story, the room usually becomes quieter. Because suddenly history no longer feels abstract. Migration becomes human. Behind every family line is often some mixture of sacrifice, uncertainty, loss, courage, and hope. And then I ask the students a question.

Almost every hand goes up. Again, almost every hand rises. Then I ask them something they do not expect: "When your children's children tell the story of your family someday, how will they tell the story of how you came to America?" The room usually grows still after that. Because most people spend little time thinking generationally. We think about survival this week, bills this month, stress this year. But very few people stop long enough to ask: what story are we building that may outlive us? That question shaped much of how we approached refugee and immigrant work over the years. We constantly reminded volunteers: think in decades. Think in generations. Not months. Not quick outcomes. Not immediate visible success. Decades. Because faithful presence is slow work. Modern culture trains us to expect rapid results. We want transformation quickly. We want measurable progress immediately. We want stories to resolve neatly within short periods of time. But human beings rarely grow that way. Trust takes time. Healing takes time. Language takes time. Belonging takes time. Community takes time. And rebuilding a life after displacement often takes far longer than outsiders realize. I remember a family — a mother and her three children — who arrived from East Africa during one of our busiest intake seasons. The first two years were extraordinarily hard. The mother worked double shifts at a food processing plant while the children navigated a school system that felt completely foreign. The oldest daughter, barely fourteen, became the family's unofficial translator — at school meetings, at doctor's appointments, at the utility company when bills came due. The weight she carried was invisible to most people around her. Three years passed before things started to stabilize. Five years before the mother was able to cut back her hours and spend evenings at home. Eight years before the oldest daughter graduated from college — the first in her family — and began working as a social worker serving newly arrived refugee families in the same city where she had once arrived with nothing. I remember the day she told me what she wanted to do with her career. I had to look away for a moment. Because I remembered the beginning. I remembered the exhaustion, the uncertainty, the long years of slow, invisible growth. And standing in front of me was evidence that the work had mattered — not on anyone's timeline, but on its own. That is one of the things long-term community work slowly teaches you. You cannot manufacture transformation on your timeline. You can only remain present faithfully enough for growth to become possible. Our culture celebrates dramatic moments. But most meaningful transformation happens quietly, over long periods of time. One conversation, one tutoring session, one meal, one ride to school. One year. Then another. Then another.

Sometimes people ask how communities change. Usually much slower than anyone hopes. And yet when you look backward after enough years, you suddenly realize everything changed. I have now lived long enough to see refugee children grow into adults. Children once struggling through basic English homework are now professionals, parents, homeowners, leaders, and mentors themselves. I have watched families who once depended on food assistance eventually start businesses and employ others. I have watched former refugees become translators helping newly arrived families navigate the same systems they once struggled to understand themselves. Those moments are deeply emotional because I remember the earlier chapters too. I often think about a simple phrase: you can count the seeds in one apple, but no one can count the apples inside one seed. That feels deeply true when working with people. We often evaluate human beings based only on what we see in the present moment — limited English, limited income, limited confidence, limited opportunity. But human potential rarely reveals itself fully at first glance. History is filled with such reminders. Albert Einstein arrived in America as a refugee fleeing Nazi Germany. Sergey Brin, co-founder of Google, immigrated as a child refugee from the Soviet Union. Steve Jobs was the son of a Syrian immigrant father. Many of the people who helped shape America across science, technology, medicine, and culture came from families who once arrived uncertain, vulnerable, and underestimated. And beyond famous names are millions of quieter stories no less meaningful. Parents sacrificing so children can flourish. Immigrants working exhausting jobs while building stability for future generations. Families creating opportunities their grandchildren may someday inherit without fully understanding the cost that made those opportunities possible. This is one reason societies must be careful how they speak about immigrants and refugees. When we reduce people to political categories, statistics, or fears, we often fail to see human potential unfolding across generations. We see only present struggle instead of future possibility. Faithful presence requires believing in that future before visible evidence fully appears. That is difficult, especially in a culture obsessed with speed and efficiency. But deep human work almost never unfolds quickly. A farmer cannot force growth by yelling at the soil. Seeds require time underground before visible life appears above the surface. Much of the most important work remains unseen for long periods. The same is true with people. You may spend years encouraging someone before confidence finally emerges. Years walking beside a family before stability begins to form. Years investing in children before their gifts fully unfold. And often the people doing faithful work never fully see the harvest themselves.

But perhaps part of maturity is learning to plant seeds for futures we may never personally control. The older I become, the more convinced I am that some of the most important work we do may only be fully understood decades later. A volunteer tutoring a struggling child today may help shape an entire future family line. A mentor encouraging one discouraged teenager may unknowingly alter the generations that follow. A community choosing welcome over fear may eventually become stronger, wiser, and more compassionate because of relationships that begin quietly now. We rarely understand fully what we are participating in while it is happening. That requires humility. It also requires hope. Hope believes growth is possible even when evidence remains incomplete. Hope plants seeds anyway. Hope keeps showing up. Hope thinks in generations. And perhaps that is one of the deepest gifts immigrant and refugee communities have given me. They reminded me that human beings are always more than their current struggle. Inside every person exists a future still unfolding. Inside every child exists possibility. Inside every family exists a story still being written. Inside every act of faithful presence exists consequences that may ripple outward long after we are gone. We can count the seeds in one apple. But no one can count the apples hidden inside one seed.

Chapter 18

The Weight of Welcome

The call came on a Tuesday afternoon, and I almost did not answer it. I had been doing this work for years by then, and I recognized the number — a caseworker from one of the resettlement agencies we partnered with. There was always something on the other end of those calls. A family in crisis. A child who had stopped attending school. A father who had lost his job and was behind on rent. An emergency that needed someone to show up. I stared at the phone for a moment longer than I should have. And then I felt something I had never quite let myself name before. I did not want to answer. Not because I did not care. I did care, deeply. But I was tired in a way that a good night's sleep could not fix. I was carrying the weight of dozens of relationships, dozens of ongoing situations, dozens of needs that never fully resolved. I had missed dinners at home. I had sat with grief I could not process because the next situation always arrived before I could finish the last one.

I answered the call. I showed up. I did what needed to be done. But that moment stayed with me for a long time. Because it forced me to reckon with something nobody in this work talks about often enough. Compassion has a cost. And if you ignore that cost long enough, it will collect on its own terms. The word for it is compassion fatigue — a very clinical phrase for something that feels much more personal. It is what happens when the weight of other people's pain accumulates faster than you are able to process it. It is not the same as burnout, though the two often travel together. Burnout is about exhaustion. Compassion fatigue is about something quieter and more erosive — a gradual numbing, a protective distance that creeps in without announcement. The calls start to feel like obligation rather than relationship. The stories start to blur together. You catch yourself hoping the next need will be simple. I have seen it happen to good people. Generous people. People who came into this work with enormous hearts and genuine love. And I have felt it in myself. I remember one particularly hard season — a winter when several families in our network were simultaneously in crisis. A domestic situation that required emergency intervention. A teenager who had been arrested. A mother who had received news from overseas that her sister had died and she had no way to grieve from ten thousand miles away. A family facing eviction. Every one of those situations was real and urgent and deserved full presence. And I was trying to hold all of them at once. My wife noticed before I did. She said I had stopped talking about the people I worked with as people. I was talking about them as problems. As situations. As cases. That stopped me cold. Because it was true. And I had not even realized it was happening. The shift from seeing people to managing problems is subtle and gradual. It does not arrive with a declaration. It creeps in through sheer volume — too many needs, too little time, too few resources, too much held too long without adequate support. I had to learn — and I am still learning — that sustainability in this work requires more than good intentions. It requires honesty about limits. It requires community. It requires people around you who will tell you the truth when you start to disappear inside the work. It requires rest. Not as weakness, but as discipline. It requires grieving what cannot be fixed. Some situations do not resolve. Some families remain in pain despite everything. Some young people do not find their way despite every effort. And carrying that without room to grieve it will hollow you out over time.

I also had to learn the difference between appropriate boundaries and self-protection that becomes indifference. That line is genuinely difficult to find. I have seen people use self-care as an excuse to stop showing up. I have also seen people destroy their health, their families, and their own humanity by refusing to acknowledge limits. The truth is probably that both errors are real, and that most people in this work swing between them. What I have come to believe is this: you cannot give from empty. You cannot love well when you have lost yourself in the process. The families we serve deserve people who are present, human, and alive — not hollow shells of people who once cared. Taking care of yourself is not a retreat from this work. It is what makes the work sustainable. The refugees and immigrants I have walked alongside for years did not need a hero. They needed neighbors. Friends. People who showed up consistently, imperfectly, and over the long term. That kind of presence is only possible when the person showing up is being nourished themselves. I eventually did learn to answer the phone with something other than dread. Not because the work became easier, but because I learned to carry it differently. I learned to ask for help. I learned to let others share the weight. I learned that I was not responsible for fixing everything — only for being faithfully present for what I could hold without losing myself in the process.

The work of welcome is holy. But it is also heavy. And perhaps the most honest thing I can say to anyone entering this kind of life is simply this: you will need more support than you think. Build it before you think you need it. Let people carry you sometimes. Stay long enough to be changed — but take care of the person who is being changed. Because the world does not need more burned-out rescuers. It needs people who have learned to love well, and then kept going.

Chapter 19

When the Story Doesn't End Well

"Not every seed we plant takes root where we can see it. But the planting still matters."

I have been trying to write this chapter for a long time. Not because I do not know what to say, but because I know exactly what to say and it is harder to write than everything else in this book. This is the chapter about the ones who did not make it. Not in death, necessarily — though there were losses like that too. I mean the ones whose stories did not resolve the way we hoped. The families that stabilized and then came apart again. The young men who drifted into situations that swallowed them. The relationships that simply faded with time and distance and unanswered calls. The moments when I looked at the distance between what I had hoped for and what actually happened, and felt the particular grief that lives in that gap. I want to tell you about a young man I will call Marcus. He arrived in America as a teenager — bright, quick to laugh, the kind of person who makes a room feel more alive. He adapted faster than most. His English came quickly. He made friends. He liked music and basketball and had a personality that drew people toward him naturally.

For several years, things went well. He graduated high school. He enrolled in a community college program.

People who knew him were quietly excited about what his life might become. And then, gradually, things began to shift. A peer group that led somewhere darker. Decisions made in moments I was not there for. A brush with the law that left consequences extending far beyond the incident itself. A stretch of months where the calls went unanswered and the silence said more than any conversation could. I kept trying. Other people kept trying. But there is a point in some relationships where showing up feels more like chasing than accompanying, and the distinction matters. You cannot want someone's future more than they are able to want it for themselves. I still do not know the full arc of Marcus's story. I hope it turns somewhere I cannot yet see. But the version I have access to does not have a tidy resolution. And I have had to learn to hold that without letting it define everything else. This kind of grief is different from ordinary grief. It is tangled up with questions I cannot answer. Did I do enough? Was there a moment I missed? Could something different have changed the outcome? Those questions rarely resolve into satisfying answers. They just have to be lived with. Alongside Marcus there were others. A family that stabilized beautifully for three years and then was torn apart by a conflict that predated America — old wounds from home that crossed the ocean and found new ground to grow in. A teenage girl who stopped coming to our programs after a falling out I never fully understood, whose number eventually became disconnected. A father whose documentation situation created a shadow over everything, whose fear eventually became isolation so complete that even people who loved him could not reach through it. None of these endings are simple. And I do not think they are meant to be. For a long time, I handled these losses poorly. I pushed through them without grieving. I moved to the next situation, the next family, the next need, and told myself that the work required resilience. That is true. But resilience without grief is not actually strength. It is avoidance in a more acceptable costume. The unprocessed grief accumulated. And it changed me in ways I did not notice until someone else named them. I had become, in certain quiet ways, more guarded. I invested a little less fully in new relationships. I held a small amount back — a self-protective instinct developed over too many goodbyes and disappointments. I told myself I was being wise. I was actually being defended. What finally helped was community — other people doing this work who were willing to say honestly that they carried the same weight. That they had also known young people who drifted beyond reach. That they had also stood at the edge of a situation with no good options and done their best anyway. That the grief was real and deserved acknowledgment and did not mean the work had failed. It helped to grieve out loud instead of silently. It helped to say: this one hurt. This one mattered. I did not get to see the ending I hoped for. And it helped to remember that I am not the author of anyone else's story. I am, at best, a participant. What I bring to a relationship matters. But it does not determine outcomes. People have agency. Lives are complex. And the same forces that can lead someone toward flourishing can, under different pressures and circumstances, lead somewhere else entirely. That is a hard thing to hold. But I think it is true. I also came to believe that even relationships that do not end well leave something behind that I cannot always measure. A person who was seen in a dark season, even if they did not respond the way I hoped, still experienced being seen. That matters even when I cannot trace its consequences. I do not say this to console myself too easily. Some situations are simply losses, and dressing them up in hopeful language can be a way of avoiding real grief. But I also do not think that every incomplete story is a failure. Sometimes seeds are planted in ground I cannot see. Sometimes the impact of faithful presence surfaces years later in ways I will never know about. I am not certain enough about any of this to state it confidently. But I hold it carefully, because the alternative — believing that every unresolved situation represents a waste — is a kind of despair I do not think is earned or useful. What I know for certain is this: the people whose stories I carry, the ones that did not resolve cleanly, changed me. Marcus changed me. The others changed me. They taught me things about human fragility and complexity and the limits of my own power that I could not have learned any other way. And the grief itself, honestly held, became its own kind of wisdom. Not a wisdom that made the loss smaller. But a wisdom that made me more human inside it. And perhaps that is what this work ultimately asks of us. Not perfect outcomes. Not tidy resolutions. Not an unbroken record of transformation. But the willingness to stay close enough to grief to be made real by it. And to keep going anyway.

Chapter 20

The Open Door

"The door you already have is the only one you need. Open it. Stay near it. See who comes."

She almost did not go. For weeks, her neighbor's door had been visible from her kitchen window. A family had moved in two months earlier — she knew they had come from somewhere far away, that they spoke little English, that they had children who played quietly near the building's entrance in the evenings. She had waved once. They had waved back. But she had not knocked. She had thought about it many times. She had even stood in her hallway once with a plate of food, fully intending to walk across the hall. And then the doubt arrived, as it always does. What would she say? What if there was a language barrier she could not cross? What if she intruded on something? What if the gesture landed strangely? What if she got it wrong? She put the plate back in the kitchen and told herself she would find a better moment. The better moment did not come on its own. It had to be chosen.

Eventually she chose it. She knocked. She held out the food — something simple she had made — and smiled. The door opened fully, and the woman on the other side smiled back. A child appeared at her knee. Another voice called something from inside the apartment. And within a few minutes she was sitting at a table she had never seen before, holding a cup of tea she had not expected, watching a family include her in something ordinary. She told me later that the fear she had spent weeks nursing dissolved within the first thirty seconds. That is almost always how it goes. I have told this kind of story many times because I believe it captures something true about the first step. The obstacle is almost never what we think it is. We imagine language barriers, cultural distance, awkwardness, complexity. Those things are real. But they are rarely as large as the fear we build around them before we begin. The hardest step is not learning a language or understanding a culture. The hardest step is the one from your door to someone else's. This book has been full of people who changed my life. Amara and her quiet dignity. Mohammed and his carried weight. The sisters from Myanmar and their patient hands. Patrick and his unshakeable faith. Ahmad calling to check on me when I was the one who was supposed to be helping. James sitting quietly in a room, waiting for someone to notice what was already inside him.

None of those relationships would exist if someone had not taken a first step toward them. And most of those first steps were ordinary. A meal dropped off. A ride offered. A name remembered. A door held open. A question asked with genuine curiosity rather than assessment. Hospitality at this level does not require a program, a budget, a nonprofit organization, or special training. It requires a decision. The decision to move toward another human being rather than away from them. That said, I do not want to make this sound simpler than it is. Cross-cultural relationships ask real things of us. They ask us to sit with misunderstanding and stay anyway. They ask us to release the need to lead every interaction or rescue every situation. They ask us to learn — not just facts about a culture or a language, but the slower, more uncomfortable learning of having our assumptions dismantled by relationship. They ask us to receive, which is often harder than giving. Many of the people I have described in this book gave me more than I gave them. That is not a comfortable thing to admit, and for a long time I was not sure what to do with it. Our cultural frameworks for this kind of engagement tend to position some people as helpers and others as helped. But real relationship does not work that way. Real relationship is mutual. It changes everyone involved.

If you want to enter this kind of life — and I believe you do, because you would not still be reading if you did not — here is what I would tell you. Start where you are. You do not need to cross an ocean. You do not need to join an organization or volunteer for a program, though both of those things are good. You need to pay attention to who is already near you. The family down the street. The coworker who eats lunch alone. The student at your child's school whose parents do not yet speak the language. The family at your place of worship who arrived six months ago and is still navigating everything alone. They are already there. They have always been there. We simply have to stop walking past them. Learn a name. That is not a small thing. In many cultures, knowing a person's name and using it correctly is one of the most significant acts of respect possible. Ask how to pronounce it. Practice until you get it right. That alone communicates: you are not interchangeable to me. You are a specific person, and I want to know you. Bring food, or accept it. The table, as this book has tried to say, is one of the oldest forms of human connection. It is almost impossible to share a meal with someone and remain a stranger to them. Eat what you are offered, even if it is unfamiliar. Cook something and bring it, even if it is imperfect. The gesture matters more than the cuisine. Stay longer than feels comfortable. Relationships in many of the cultures represented in our immigrant and refugee communities are built on time — unhurried, ungoverned by clocks. If you show up for thirty minutes and leave, it communicates a different value system than sitting for two hours because the conversation was good. You do not have to abandon your schedule entirely. But stretching it occasionally communicates that the relationship is worth more than your next task. And return. Go back. Consistency is everything. A single visit is kindness. A pattern of visits is belonging. The families I have known who integrated most fully into American life did so not because of any single intervention but because of people who kept showing up. Month after month. Year after year. Through awkwardness and breakthroughs and long stretches of ordinary life. You will get things wrong. You will say something that does not land the way you meant it. You will misread a situation. You will bring the wrong food, arrive at the wrong time, make assumptions that turn out to be embarrassingly incorrect. This is not a reason to stop. It is evidence that you are actually in a real relationship, which always involves error and repair. The door at the end of this book is the same door it has always been. It is the door you already have. The one that opens onto your street, your neighborhood, your city, your ordinary life. Leave it open.

Leave it open long enough for someone to notice that you mean it. And then wait — not passively, but with the active patience of someone who has decided that what comes through that door is worth more than whatever you were doing before. The stranger is not a disruption to your life. They are an invitation into a larger one. And the only thing standing between you and that larger life is the decision to open the door — and then to stay on the other side of it long enough to find out who you were meant to become.

Conclusion

The Gift of Guests

"May our capacity to love keep expanding—without judgment, without condition, and without needing to control the outcome."

By now, you have met many people. You have listened to stories of forgiveness that did not erase pain, but refused to let it harden the heart. You have watched listening take place across language barriers and cultural distance. You have seen vulnerability practiced under pressure, dignity honored in small things, hope grow slowly in shattered lives, belonging take shape through consistency, burdens shared when weight became too heavy to carry alone, hospitality offered without abundance, and faith endure when everything else fell away. None of these lessons arrived as arguments. They arrived as people. And that, I have come to believe, is not accidental. Over the years, my own faith has been slowly reshaped by a quieter practice—one often described as contemplation. I've learned to think of it less as a technique and more as a posture. A way of paying attention. A willingness to slow down long enough to see what is real.

To see myself honestly—my fears, biases, and blind spots. To see others as they truly are—bearers of dignity, created in the image of God. To see God not as an idea to defend, but as a presence to receive. To see creation in its beauty and fragility. To see suffering without turning away. At its heart, contemplation is about learning how to see. Scripture returns to this theme again and again. Jesus often spoke of sight not merely as physical ability, but as spiritual perception. 'Those who have eyes to see, let them see.' He healed blindness not only to restore vision, but to reveal how easily we look without truly noticing. The psalmist prays, 'Open my eyes, that I may see.' Paul writes of eyes being 'opened' to grasp hope and truth. Seeing, in the biblical imagination, is not passive. It is moral. It changes us. That kind of seeing has shaped this book. Because when we slow down long enough to really see immigrants—not as categories or problems, but as people—something begins to shift. We notice courage where we expected weakness. Generosity where we assumed scarcity. Faith where we anticipated fear. We begin to see imago Dei—the image of God—where it has too often been obscured. This is where the ancient word philoxenia returns one final time. Often translated as hospitality, philoxenia comes from two Greek words: phileo—love, and xenos—stranger or guest. Literally, it means love of the stranger. Or even more plainly, love of the guest. This is not sentimental language. The Christian call to hospitality was never about entertaining friends or hosting people like us. It was about cultivating a way of seeing that refuses fear and resists dehumanization. It was about recognizing the presence of God in the other. Philoxenia is not an emotion. It is a posture. It does not require agreement. It does not erase difference. It does not demand perfection. It simply asks us to see—and then to respond. One of the quiet lies many people believe is that meaningful engagement with immigrants requires extraordinary capacity. That you must have special training, endless time, or the ability to solve enormous problems. When the needs feel overwhelming, withdrawal can seem like the only honest response. But what this book has shown—again and again—is that transformation rarely begins with grand gestures. It begins with attention. With noticing who is already around you. With listening before labeling. With learning one story before forming one opinion. With staying present when it would be easier to move on. Hospitality does not ask you to fix what you did not break. It asks you to see what you have been trained to overlook.

There are practical ways this posture can take shape in ordinary lives. Pay attention to the people already in your orbit—neighbors, coworkers, parents at school events. Practice listening without rushing to interpret or correct. Learn names. Remember them. Support local organizations already doing the work of welcome. Allow relationships to form at the pace trust requires. Be willing to receive, not just give. None of these require expertise.

They require attentiveness. And attentiveness changes us. One of the most consistent themes throughout these chapters is reversal. Again and again, the assumed roles shift. The helper becomes the one helped. The teacher becomes the student. The guest becomes the one who offers the gift. This is not weakness. It is formation. Immigrants do not need to be idealized to be honored. They do not need to be perfect to be worthy of dignity. What they offer us—often without intending to—is a mirror. They help us see what forgiveness looks like when it is costly. What listening looks like when misunderstanding is constant. What faith looks like when it is stripped of comfort and control. What hospitality looks like when there is little to spare. They remind us of ways of being human that many of us have slowly lost—not because we are cruel, but because we are distracted. In a culture shaped by fear of the other, they invite us back to courage. In a society obsessed with speed and productivity, they invite us back to presence. In a world addicted to control, they invite us back to trust. Philoxenia is not naïve. It knows the world is complex. It does not deny the need for wisdom, boundaries, or law. But it insists that love must remain at the center—or everything else becomes hollow. To love the guest is not to surrender discernment. It is to refuse blindness. And that refusal matters. Because when we learn to see immigrants not as threats to manage, but as neighbors to know, something begins to change—not just in our opinions, but in our hearts. We become slower to judge. Quicker to listen. More honest about our fears. More aware of our shared vulnerability. The gift of the guest is not that they make our lives easier. It is that they teach us how to see again. This book does not end with a solution, because hospitality is not a project with an endpoint. It is a practice—a way of inhabiting the world that must be chosen again and again. But if there is one thing worth carrying forward, it is this: You do not need to see everything at once. You only need to be willing to look more truthfully. And in doing so, you may discover what generations before us knew well—that sometimes, the stranger is not a disruption to our faith. Sometimes, the stranger is the one who restores our sight.

Practical Ways to Welcome Refugees and New Neighbors

Many people want to help refugees and immigrants but feel unsure where to begin. They imagine they need special training, large amounts of money, or extraordinary qualifications. But most meaningful hospitality begins through ordinary human presence. Small acts matter. Consistent acts matter even more. Here are ten practical ways anyone can begin creating belonging within their own community. 1. Learn Someone's Story Before Forming an Opinion Most people know immigration as a political topic before they know immigrants as human beings. Slow down long enough to listen. Ask questions. Be curious. Learn where someone came from, what they experienced, what they hope for, and what challenges they face. Stories humanize people in ways headlines never can. 2. Share a Meal Together Few things build trust faster than eating together. Invite someone into your home. Accept invitations into theirs. Bring food. Stay longer than feels efficient.

The table has a unique ability to turn strangers into neighbors. 3. Volunteer Consistently, Not Occasionally One-time events can help, but long-term relationships change lives. Children especially need stable adults who continue showing up. Consistency builds trust. Even a few hours a month over several years can make a profound difference. Think in decades, not moments. 4. Help With Practical Needs Without Creating Dependency Many refugee families need help navigating systems that longtime residents take for granted. Transportation. Practicing

English.

School forms.

Learning

Job public applications. transportation.

Understanding healthcare systems. Offer help in ways that build confidence and dignity rather than control. The goal is empowerment, not saviorism. 5. Become Comfortable Crossing Cultural Differences You will eventually misunderstand something. That is normal. Approach differences with humility instead of fear. Most people extend grace when they sense genuine respect and openness.

Curiosity builds bridges faster than perfection. 6. Invest in Children and Teenagers Refugee youth often adapt quickly outwardly while carrying enormous internal pressures. Mentor. Tutor. Coach. Encourage. Listen. Children remember adults who consistently believed in them. Sometimes one caring adult can alter the trajectory of a young person's life. 7. Support Refugee-Owned Businesses Eat at immigrant restaurants. Hire refugee entrepreneurs. Recommend their services. Buy their products. Economic dignity matters deeply. Every purchase can become an act of encouragement and belonging. 8. Teach Your Children to Move Toward Difference, Not Fear It Children learn openness or suspicion largely from adults. Expose them to different cultures. Different foods. Different stories. Different friendships. Help them see people as human beings before categories. Hospitality often begins at home. 9. Stay Long Enough to Build Real Relationships

Many people enjoy helping briefly but disappear when relationships become complicated, slow, or inconvenient. But trust grows slowly. Real community requires endurance. Stay long enough to know birthdays, graduations, struggles, celebrations, disappointments, and growth over time. Faithful presence changes people. Including you. 10. Remember That Refugees Are Not Projects — They Are Neighbors People do not primarily need to feel "helped." They need to feel seen. Known. Respected. Included. Approach relationships with mutuality. You are not only bringing something valuable into the relationship. You are also receiving something valuable from it. Hospitality changes both the guest and the host. And often the people we think we are serving end up teaching us how to become more human ourselves.

Acknowledgments

This book would not exist without the generosity of the many people who have shared their lives, their stories, and their tables with me. I am deeply grateful to the immigrants and refugees whose courage, wisdom, and hospitality have shaped every page of this work. Though many names have been changed to protect privacy, you know who you are — and I am better for having known you. To my family — thank you for your patience, your love, and your willingness to share me with this work. You are my first and greatest gift. To the colleagues, mentors, and communities who have walked alongside me in this work — your faithfulness and friendship have made this possible. And to everyone who has ever opened a door — literally or figuratively — thank you for showing the rest of us what it looks like.

About the Author

Joel Vestal is a humanitarian, speaker, nonprofit leader, and storyteller whose life and work have been shaped by decades of cross-cultural relationships, global travel, and community engagement. Through work with refugees, immigrants, vulnerable communities, and nonprofit initiatives both in the United States and internationally, he has spent much of his life helping create spaces of belonging, dignity, and hospitality. Having traveled to more than 70 countries and lived among diverse cultures around the world, Joel writes with a deep belief that human beings are transformed not only by serving others but also by learning to truly see them. His work explores themes of hospitality, resilience, faith, cultural understanding, compassion, emotional healing, and the shared humanity that exists beneath fear and division. Joel has worked extensively with refugee and immigrant families, helping communities build long-term relationships across cultural, religious, and linguistic differences. His writing combines personal stories, reflective insight, spiritual depth, and practical wisdom, shaped by years of walking alongside people as they rebuild their lives after displacement, loss, and transition. In The Gift of Guests, Joel invites readers to rediscover hospitality not merely as entertaining people, but as allowing relationships to reshape the heart.

Joel is married and the father of two twenty-something children. He continues to write, speak, mentor, and create content centered on hope, healing, faith, and human dignity in a fragmented world. You can find Joel on most social media platforms or at joelvestal.com. You can find Joel on most social media platforms or at joelvestal.com.

www.ingramcontent.com/pod-product-compliance
Lightning Source LLC
LaVergne TN
LVHW090613110826
845146LV00001B/372

* 9 7 9 8 9 9 6 1 4 2 7 3 6 *